The Myers–Briggs Type Indicator ®

The Myers–Briggs Type Indicator®

A CRITICAL REVIEW AND PRACTICAL GUIDE

Rowan Bayne

Department of Psychology
University of East London
London
UK

CHAPMAN & HALL

London · Glasgow · Weinheim · New York · Tokyo · Melbourne · Madras

Published by Chapman & Hall, 2–6 Boundary Row, London SE1 8HN, UK

Chapman & Hall, 2–6 Boundary Row, London SE1 8HN, UK

Blackie Academic & Professional, Wester Cleddens Road, Bishopbriggs, Glasgow G64 2NZ, UK

Chapman & Hall GmbH, Pappelallee 3, 69469 Weinheim, Germany

Chapman & Hall USA, One Penn Plaza, 41st Floor, New York NY 10119, USA

Chapman & Hall Japan, ITP-Japan, Kyowa Building, 3F, 2–2–1 Hirakawacho, Chiyoda-ku, Tokyo 102, Japan

Chapman & Hall Australia, Thomas Nelson Australia, 102 Dodds Street, South Melbourne, Victoria 3205, Australia

Chapman & Hall India, R. Seshadri, 32 Second Main Road, CIT East, Madras 600 035, India

Distributed in the USA and Canada by Singular Publishing Group Inc., 4284 41st Street, San Diego, California 92105

First edition 1995

© 1995 Rowan Bayne

Typeset in 10/12 Times by Saxon Graphics Ltd, Derby
Printed and bound in Great Britain by Hartnolls Ltd, Bodmin

ISBN 0 412 57460 8   1 56593 353 2 (USA)

A catalogue record for this book is available from the British Library

♾ Printed on permanent acid-free text paper, manufactured in accordance with ANSI/NISO Z39.48–1992 and ANSI/NISO Z39.48–1984 (Permanence of Paper).

For Linda Robinson,
ISTJ and proud of it.

Contents

Acknowledgements

I'd like to thank all the people who have contributed to this book, particularly Jan Woodley, Tony Merry, Chris Lewis and Richard Kwiatkowski for their helpful comments on drafts of some or all the chapters and Susamma Ajith for wordprocessing with skill, patience and speed. My warm thanks too, to Rosemary Morris (editor), Helen Heyes (sub-editor), Holly Regan-Jones (copy-editor) and other staff at Chapman & Hall who have helped produce the book.

Parts of Chapters 2 and 7 are from a paper in the *British Journal of Guidance and Counselling* (Bayne, in press) and are used here with permission. Other copyright acknowledgements are included in the text, except for several articles by myself in the *Newsletter of the British Association for Psychological Type*, which I've drawn on but not cited. I'd like to thank the editors, Merilyn Parker and (currently) Peter Naylor, for their support and editorial skills.

Rowan Bayne
August 1994

Introduction and overview

This book has two aims: to critically review the widely used but much-criticized Myers–Briggs Type Indicator (MBTI) and to outline and discuss some of the MBTI's applications in counselling, education, management and training. I examine the main underlying ideas and some of the best research and I try to spell out how the MBTI and Myers' psychological type theory can be most useful.

I wrote the book with several groups of people in mind:

- people who know their MBTI results or their psychological type (in Myers' sense);
- psychology students and others studying personality as part of a course. The book offers a viewpoint on some of the basic issues in personality as well as concentrating on the MBTI;
- anyone puzzled by and interested in themselves and others. The MBTI is an unusually positive and constructive approach;
- students and practitioners looking for a worthwhile research project in applied personality theory;
- my colleagues – counsellors, psychologists, teachers, health professionals and managers.

OVERVIEW OF THE THEORY

It may be helpful as a prelude or a 'refresher' to read the following overview of Myers' theory or an introductory text, e.g. Kroeger and Thuesen (1988) or Hirsh and Kummerow (1989).

Psychological type is Myers' (1980) clarification and development of part of Jung's theory of personality. Myers suggested 16 'kinds of people', describing all 16 primarily in terms of strengths and potential strengths. The central concept is **preference**, which means 'feeling most comfortable and natural with'. The theory assumes that each of us prefers some ways of behaving to others and that there are four main choices in this respect. These are between:

Extraversion (E)	and	introversion (I)
Sensing (S)	and	intuition (N)
Thinking (T)	and	feeling (F)
Judging (J)	and	perceiving (P).

MBTI results indicate a provisional type composed of one from each of these pairs of preferences, e.g. ISFJ, ENFJ. There are 16 such combinations or psychological types. The four pairs of preferences are discussed in Chapter 2 and the idea of 'type' in Chapter 3, as the next section shows.

OVERVIEW OF THE BOOK

Chapter 1 answers the question 'Why type theory?'. I discuss eight positive characteristics of psychological type theory and the MBTI, but if your main interest is in what the MBTI measures and how it is used, you may wish to begin with Chapter 2 or one of the applications chapters.

Chapter 2 focuses on the meaning and validity of the basic level of the MBTI: the four pairs of preferences. I discuss ways of helping someone discover and check their psychological type; the main sources of evidence on the validity of the MBTI; and what is known and not known about each of the preferences.

Chapter 3 is about two more complex levels of type theory: interactions between the preferences to create – or claim to create – the sixteen types and 'type dynamics'. I also touch on a simpler level, called temperament theory.

Chapter 4 reviews type's model of lifelong personality development. I discuss the concepts of 'good' and 'false' type development and the questions of whether type development should and can be speeded up and how it might be measured. The second half of this chapter is an analysis of her own development as an ESTJ by Dr Jean Kummerow.

Chapter 5 outlines and replies to ten criticisms of the MBTI and type theory and nine questions about them.

Chapter 6 discusses several obstacles to observing type accurately in everyday life and suggests strategies for countering them.

Chapters 7, 8 and 9 focus on three areas of application – counselling, education and management, respectively. Ideas and evidence are reviewed on type and such topics as empathy, personality change, learning style, writing, the 'good manager' and coping with stress.

Chapter 10 is for MBTI trainers. It suggests some principles to take into account in designing MBTI training and outlines exercises on several aspects of type. I also emphasize, however, that this is an approach which works for me and (type's central theme) that there are several other radically different, equally valid ways of behaving and being.

Why psychological type?

There are many theories of personality and even more measures. What's more, type sounds like astrology and stereotyping, so – why psychological type? In this chapter, I discuss eight positive aspects of Isabel Myers' theory. Some of these aspects can also be seen as weaknesses and I consider criticisms of type and of the MBTI both here and – primarily – in Chapter 5. The eight aspects are:

1. the aims of type theory and the MBTI;
2. the tone of type descriptions;
3. the concept of preference;
4. the concept of type;
5. a 'twist' in the descriptions of the types;
6. type's model of lifelong personality development;
7. the MBTI itself;
8. the history of the MBTI.

The concept of preference is discussed at greater length than the other seven aspects. I compare it with Rogers' self theory of personality, in particular his two concepts of actualization of the real self and congruence. Tougher-minded concepts are also clearly related to preference, for example assertiveness, which is usually claimed by the cognitive–behavioural approach to personality and counselling (Rakos, 1991).

THE AIMS OF TYPE THEORY AND THE MBTI

Type theory has three general aims, to do with self, others and self-development respectively. The first aim is to help people identify or confirm the ways in which they – and their 'kind of person' – are likely to be most effective and most fulfilled. Type seeks to help people clarify what 'suits' them and to value it, usually by bringing aspects of themselves into focus in a reframing or confirming way rather than by dramatic revelation. One of the points of discovering, or deciding on, a type that fits is that it offers new insights, e.g. 'Perhaps as an introvert I really do need to spend more time on my own, for everyone's sake', or 'I tend to work in bursts because I prefer intuition and it's OK to be like that' – both examples at the simplest level of type (Chapter 2).

One leading figure in type research, Tom Carskadon, said (as an early reaction to his MBTI results): 'It seemed to say an awful lot about me that I didn't think I'd told it'. I find the sceptical note here appealing, but his main point underlines type's first aim: to provide an economical summary of central aspects of personality, one which increases self-understanding and implies certain ways of being and behaving more than others. Moreover, by identifying these central characteristics we can make useful guesses about numerous other, more specific personal qualities.

On re-reading Carskadon's remark, it can be interpreted as threatened – the MBTI as X-ray or stereotype psychoanalyst. In context, Carskadon was being enthusiastic, as you might expect from the Editor of *The Journal of Psychological Type*. My early experience was similar: the MBTI told me more than I told it and I felt more comfortable with parts of myself, encouraged and stimulated. Moreover, I have continued to discover new aspects of myself and type in the subsequent 13 or 14 years.

Type thus implies a principle: that people identify what they are best at and do it most of the time. It focuses on fairly general characteristics, at the level of 'how your mind works' rather than specific talents or expressions of strengths, and is therefore a step towards understanding individuality, rather than about individuality itself. In Jung's phrase, it provides 'compass points in the wilderness of the psyche'.

The second aim is to help people understand and value others more, especially those of very different types from oneself – or at least to be more ready to see them as different rather than odd, weird or wrong. Myers' main concern in developing type theory was to encourage the 'constructive use of differences'. Differences in type can lead to misunderstanding and hostility. Opposite types can be the enemy! (So can the same type, but less often and for different reasons.) Myers wanted people to value the opposite preferences to their own. For example, one student, an extravert, used to dismiss introverts as dull and boring; now, after working on type theory, she sees them as inclined to reflection and as liking more time alone than she does. She now often writes notes to an introverted colleague rather than expecting an immediate discussion.

Allport (1961a), writing in general terms, not about type, suggested that 'Much of our lives is spent in trying to understand others (and in wishing others understood us better than they do). Our chief effort is to grasp correctly the motives and intentions of the other, for we would then know the guidelines of his life' (p. 520). Even those people less interested in others' motives and guidelines than psychologists are, find other people baffling sometimes: type is a way of understanding them better and in a constructive way. Person X, who probably prefers thinking and judging, may not mean it personally when she criticizes you or ignores your needs. Rather, that's how she most comfortably sees the world and (in many circumstances a major strength) she tends to be task-focused.

The third aim of type theory is to help people understand key aspects of the development of their personality throughout life. MBTI results and their interpretation at one level help people understand and value their type, and at another level suggest possible areas for development. The sections in this chapter on the 'twist' in type and on development touch on this third aim while Chapter 4 explores it in more detail.

THE TONE OF TYPE DESCRIPTIONS

Type theory tries to achieve its aims through the accuracy of its descriptions and through their positive tone. The descriptions of each type are glowing. A colleague referred to them as 'vignettes of unrelenting virtue', meaning they are too good to be true. In the sense that type doesn't describe the whole of personality, he was right.

The positive tone was not easily achieved. Lawrence (1989) gave the example (Table 1.1) of successive attempts to describe part of thinking.

Table 1.1: An example of trying to avoid biased language in type descriptions (from Lawrence, 1989)

'Thinking types are relatively unemotional ... may seem hard-hearted.' (Myers, 1962)

Became

'... do not show emotion readily ... tend to be firm-minded.' (Myers, 1976)

Became

'... respond more to people's ideas than their feelings.' (Hammer, 1987)

The first two attempts were by Myers, an INFP and therefore, in theory, with thinking least developed. Her second version was in response to comments from people who prefer thinking and the third and current version is by Hammer, an INTP. (The dominant function of INTPs is thinking and therefore he should, in theory, be more likely to understand developed thinking.)

THE CONCEPT OF PREFERENCE

The concept of preference is at the heart of the MBTI and the underlying theory. It can be defined as 'feeling most natural and comfortable with', but there is no formal definition in the MBTI literature and it is perhaps best defined by analogy. The analogy most often used is handedness, but crossing your arms or legs, clasping your hands or catching a ball also make the point. Each action usually feels more natural and comfortable carried out one way than it does carried out the other way.

Table 1.2: Representative results of handedness exercise (as analogy for preference)

Preferred hand	Non-preferred hand
Comfortable	Awkward
Natural	Clumsy
Easy	Childlike
Flowing	Much harder
Automatic	Timid
Confident	Slow
	Wobbly
	Had to concentrate
	Embarrassing

Table 1.2 illustrates common responses in workshops to the exercise of writing your signature first as you usually do and then with your other hand. Comfortableness and greater competence tend to go together, but sometimes the outcome with the non-preferred hand is better, at least in some respects, e.g. a more legible signature.

There are two main points here. First, while we *can* use our non-preferred hand, generally we don't and if we do, it takes more concentration and effort and is therefore more tiring and harder to sustain. Second, preferences are strongly related to behaviour but not identical with it. Table 1.3 lists some of the factors affecting behaviour. For example, the MBTI doesn't attempt to measure several important individual differences, e.g. anxiety or type development. Behaviour is multiply caused. Preferences, and how developed they are, are main influences, in some situations more than others, but they are not the whole of personality and are far from being the only factors in understanding experience and behaviour.

There is a potential problem with the preferences not being the same as behaviour : there needs to be a substantial relationship between preferences and behaviour or the theory becomes empty, explaining everything and therefore nothing. Taking someone's sensitive intervention, for example, you could say he prefers feeling or, if you later discover he's a thinking type, that he has

Table 1.3: Some of the factors influencing behaviour

Psychological type (preferences)

Type development

Other personality characteristics

Motives

Situations

Roles

Health

Mood

Stress

Chance

---

well-developed feeling. This 'hedging of bets' – at least in so bald a form – would be antiscientific. However, type's relationship with behaviour *is* substantial, as discussed later.

In the rest of this section, three main sets of questions are considered:

1. Does the idea of preferences being 'natural' make sense? Here preference is compared with the rather vague notions of real self and actualization of the real self. However, these seem to me to be concepts that keep reappearing in psychology (with different names, e.g. autonomy, congruence, assertiveness) because they are about a fundamental tension in each person: a need to 'be ourselves' versus a need to behave in line with roles and expectations.
2. What is the **content** of the real self? (The preferences are one possibility.) And what is the origin of the real self and the preferences? Are they inherited? What is the role of the environment?
3. What is the **incidence** of actualization of the real self (or assertiveness or type development), i.e. do most people develop their preferences to at least a reasonable extent and more than their non-preferences?

Preferences: what does 'natural' mean?

One objection to the idea of preference is that 'natural' is a dangerous word, too glibly associated with 'good'. Conversely, learned behaviour which is 'unnatural' is too glibly associated with 'bad'. Let's take as a starting point a provocative experiment by Davis (1928), recently re-examined by Galef (1991). Davis allowed three newly weaned infants to eat whatever they liked, from a large selection, at every meal. The infants were eight, nine and ten months old. For two of them the experiment lasted six months and for the other a year. All the foods were 'natural' – no milk products, no canned food. The experiment was very carefully carried out. For my purposes here, the following results matter most:

1. After the first few meals the infants chose their food without difficulty. They spat some foods out early on but learned to recognize the foods quickly and know what and how much they wanted. They ate salt occasionally, spluttering and even crying, but never spitting it out and often going back for more.
2. The infants chose balanced diets but *not* balanced meals. For example, one of them ate seven eggs on one occasion, another four bananas.
3. They did not suffer from stomach pains or constipation. They were judged to be happy and active and they gained height and weight well.

There are two minor qualifications of the results: the foods were natural and the meals were at set times, so the results do not tell us what would have happened if ice-cream, chocolate cake, etc. had been available or if the infants had eaten whenever they wished.

The results are useful as a metaphor, whether they are literally true or not (Galef, 1991). However, they do tell us that the infants in some way knew what they wanted and acted accordingly. They had preferences for different foods and acted on them. Their potential in terms of height and weight, health and perhaps activity level was actualized to at least a significant extent. In Rogers' (1961) phrase they were in this respect 'exquisitely rational'.

However, many people eat for reasons other than hunger and even when they are hungry, eat foods which they do not really want. This suggests a distinction between real, authentic needs and false, inauthentic ones, e.g. I crave some chocolate cake when sometimes what I really want is, say, exercise, a hug or some sleep. The distinction between 'real' and 'false' is central to the concept of preference, even though false needs and selves have a reality in their own right and the term 'false' is therefore awkward.

What about preferences in the form of other needs and qualities? Hunger is vital to survival and stimulated by tissue deficits, while most needs are not. Here I find Rogers' (e.g. 1964) concept of the Organismic Valuing Process (OVP) helpful. He argues that we introject values without considering them or making them our own. The result is inner conflict between the OVP – our capacity to recognize our wishes and needs – and the introjected values and the result of that is that we tend to lose touch, to some extent, with our OVP.

However, adults can use their OVPs in a more complex way and on a far wider range of decisions than infants use theirs. In particular, our OVPs can take into account relevant memories and ideas, for example about consequences for ourselves and others. The OVP is also – when used properly – self-correcting, much as our kinesthetic sense gives feedback to help us stand and walk. When we have a decision to make, e.g. shall I go out with X tonight?, what Rogers suggests *can* happen is that the various factors (I want to watch TV, X will be disappointed if I don't go, etc.) are weighed and the OVP suggests the best decision at the moment. What actually tends to happen, according to Rogers, is that the OVP is not consulted and – at the expense of one part of ourselves – we do something we do not really want to and thus in some degree fail to actualize our preferences.

At this point I come to more formal definitions of real self and actualization of the real self. I see self as depicted in Figure 1.1, which is an interpretation of Rogers' theory. Actualization of the real self is a combination of experience (level 1), being aware of it (level 2) and, as much as is appropriate, behaving accordingly (level 3).

The phrase 'as much as is appropriate' is vague. It can be seen in terms of a threshold amount of actualization (say, two hours per person per day) or a favourable ratio of actualizing behaviours to those which are not. Actualization of the real self occurs when organismic experience is (a) present in awareness and (b) communicated. Three levels are thus involved and two overlapping definitions – when all three levels are congruent and when levels 1 and 2 are. More succinctly, it is 'congruence between levels of personality when the organismic level is one of them'. Measurement of such a concept is discussed in Bayne (1977).

It is also worth emphasizing – as Rogers does – the difference between being aware of potential (and perhaps speaking about it) on the one hand and acting on awareness on the other. They are radically different. To take an extreme example, it is one thing to feel a murderous impulse and/or to speak about it, another to kill someone.

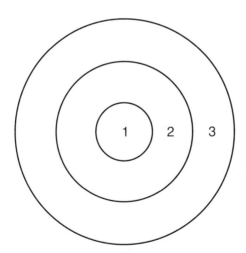

1 = 'Real self', including Organismic Valuing Process (OVP)
2 = Awareness, including self-concept
3 = Behaviour

Figure 1.1 Three levels of personality.

McCrae and Costa (in press) suggest the following elements of a complete personality theory:

- basic tendencies, which includes the preferences of type theory, the factors of their own five factor theory and the organismic self of Rogers' theory;
- characteristic adaptations, defined as 'the concrete manifestations of basic tendencies', e.g. acquired skills and habits – questionnaires like the MBTI use questions about characteristic adaptations to make inferences about basic tendencies;
- the self-concept – 'knowledge, views, and evaluations of the self';
- the 'objective biography' – everything experienced or done by a person;
- external influences.

The five elements are outlined in Figure 1.2.

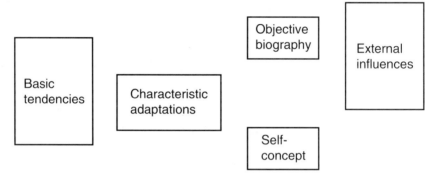

Figure 1.2 Five elements of a comprehensive personality theory (from McCrae and Costa (in press)).

In broad terms, there is a clear correspondence between this model of personality and type theory, though McCrae and Costa have spelled their model out much more clearly. Nevertheless, they refer to it as a 'sketch' and 'desperately in need of elaboration'. How, for example, do characteristic adaptations develop? Are most basic tendencies fully developed by about 30 years of age, as McCrae and Costa suggest (with supporting evidence), or is there some truth in Jung's lifelong model of personality development? And what are the processes linking each of the elements?

Content and origin of the real self and the preferences

The most obvious content of level 1 (Figure 1.1) is 'real feelings, wants, reactions, thoughts and sensations'. Several personality theorists argue by analogy from simpler life forms. Thus Maslow used oak trees and tigers to illustrate his views, and Jung used lions and crocodiles; Rogers cited potatoes, seaweed and lions; while Perls chose elephants, eagles and wheat. For example, Perls (1969) argued that eagles actualize their real selves by roaming the sky and building a particular kind of nest and that elephants actualize a quite different potential or real self. In this analogy only humans (and perhaps a few pets and other captive animals) have the capacity *not* to actualize themselves.

Some theorists include individual differences as part of level 1 in people. Storr (1960), for example, suggested that an extraverted child brought up to be introverted might recover its 'constitutional extraversion' through therapy. In other words, he suggests that some people's potential predisposes them towards extraversion. Of course, Jung and others have suggested further characteristics which can be submerged – rather than destroyed – if a person's early life is sufficiently discouraging. Rogers avoids discussing this aspect of content, perhaps for philosophical reasons. Presumably whether traits, talents, capacities, etc. develop or not depends on (a) how robust they are and (b) how encouraging or otherwise the environment is.

The MBTI assumes that four pairs of preferences are particularly important. Taking one of these as an example, type theory suggests that some people prefer extraversion and generally find that behaving in an extraverted way is more comfortable for them than introversion, while other people prefer introversion. The MBTI sets out to measure preferences only, not how well or poorly developed those preferences are.

The research most relevant to the origins of the preferences is on identical twins who were separated early (at an average of six weeks old) and brought up by different families (Bouchard *et al.*, 1990; Bergeman *et al.*, 1993). The twins' scores on many ability and personality tests are closer than would be expected if the same person took the test twice. In addition, Bouchard *et al.* (1990) found some striking similarities between some of the twins. For example, two male twins separated at four weeks old and not meeting until they were 40 had both been deputy sheriffs and petrol station attendants and both enjoyed carpentry. They drank the same beer and smoked the same cigarettes. More extraordinary, they had both married women called Linda, divorced them and remarried women called Betty. However, the choice of names is hardly likely to be genetic in origin and suggests rather the influence of similar environments and the role of coincidence.

One problem with interpreting such similarities is a statistical one. Unusual things inevitably happen sometimes, because so many things happen. When 1000 things happen, one of them is the one in 1000 remarkable thing. If a number of pairs of unrelated people are compared on enough characteristics there will be some similarities. So the problem is to try and tease out the effects of environment, genes and chance.

One line of evidence is to compare identical and non-identical twins. For example, identical twins reared apart are more alike in height than are non-identical twins reared apart, despite the role of nutrition and other environmental factors. Therefore genes contribute substantially to height. Does the same logic apply to personality characteristics like the preferences?

Apart from broad statements, for example that the environment interacts with genetic predispositions to enhance or impede their expression, we don't yet know. There are several complicating factors. The first is a technical principle in genetics. The genes which influence height are additive. Each one either adds to or subtracts from the effects of the others. But genes can also interact with each other, so that only the right combination will lead to a particular character-istic. The odds against a particular combination occurring might be very long indeed and are thought to explain rare abilities in music or mathematics as well as characteristics like extraversion (Lykken *et al.*, 1992).

Second, there is an environmental explanation for the remarkable similarities in personality. The striking physical similarities of identical twins reared apart may lead to similar treatment and therefore to similarity of personality, interests, etc. Physical attractiveness is certainly a factor in how others behave towards us (Feingold, 1992). The evidence for an effect on personality is less clear.

Third, identical twins tend to be matched in terms of social class, nationality, etc. with their foster parents and thus their environments may not differ very much. Similarly, some twins are not separated very early; for example, Lykken *et al.* (1992) quote a 1988 study of 315 pairs of twins reared apart since they were ten years old. Environmental and genetic influences were far from sepa-rate in this study.

Bergeman *et al.* (1993) studied three of the Big Five personality factors (related to SN, TF and JP in the MBTI and discussed in Chapter 2) in twins who were separated at an average age of 2.8 years. They found little effect of degree of separation and concluded that in general:

> A very broad range of personality traits have been shown to be substan-tially influenced by genetic factors, and relatively unaffected by shared environmental factors. When it is recalled that the 'shared rearing envi-ronmental factors' include such influences as parents' style of child-rear-ing, socioeconomic status, religious training, educational opportunities, and neighbourhood peer groups, this is an astounding fact. (p. 173)

The concept of different behaviours being 'constitutionally right' for each person seems to me both appealing and disturbing. In the very act of providing an apparently real basis for self-definition or identity it also sets limits to how much we can change. For type theory, it is a reasonable working hypothesis that the preferences and types are genetic predispositions.

Incidence of actualization of the real self and type development

Many of the theorists cited above – Rogers, Maslow, Perls – see people generally as self-alienated rather than self-actualizing. They contrast those people who are relatively aware of their real feelings with the majority who are not. In terms of behaviour rather than kinds of people, they state that some behaviour is self-actu-alizing and most is false. Like psychoanalysts, they think that subtle techniques are needed to discover what people are really thinking and feeling. On the other side of this contest are personality theorists who believe that most people are, as it were, incorrigibly themselves and thus able, if they wish, to answer straightforward questionnaires accurately as a matter of course. Allport (1953), Myers (1980) and McCrae and Costa (in press) represent this view.

Consider an example from a novel, which falls firmly on the Rogers/Maslow side. Gébler (1969) wrote, using the term 'men' to mean 'people':

> Most men spend their lives pretending to be someone else. A bank manager could hardly be said to be truly himself. He's trapped in somebody else's clothes. He says 'I'll attend to your needs immediately Mr Profit', when he is longing to leap over the counter and defecate on his head.

Such a passage is provocative to personality researchers as well as bank managers and customers. A number of points can be made. For example, if we want to predict how the bank manager will behave, then he actually does smile and does not leap over the counter. His 'real feelings' may therefore be irrelevant. As Sechrest puts it: 'At some point the underlying elements, the structure of the personality, the conflicts, must articulate with the ongoing behaviour of the individual. Otherwise they lose all meaning ... the question of the underlying personality, of what a person is really like, becomes trivial' (Sechrest, 1968, p. 530).

However, the phrase 'at some point' is crucial. If Rogers' and Maslow's theories are valid, the bank manager's behaviour (and experience) will be affected: he will at some point experience himself as inauthentic, perhaps suffer from headaches, lack zest and so on. Type theory adds a further element: some types are naturally comfortable with the behaviour expected of bank managers and are truly themselves in that role.

Actualization of one's real self and type development could be 'patchy' rather than all or nothing. Both sides of the controversy may be right either for different elements in the content of organismic experience or for different kinds of people. In the latter case, those people whose behaviour represents them authentically are actualizing their real selves and those for whom it is a mask are not. As Allport (1961b) commented: 'Psychology urgently needs to make a distinction between lives in which the existential layer is, in effect, the whole of the personality, and other lives in which it is a mere mask for the rumblings of the unconscious'. However, both sides cannot be right about the incidence. The validity evidence for the MBTI, discussed in Chapters 2 and 3, seems to me to support the more optimistic views of Allport, Myers and McCrae and Costa. I discuss this issue further in Chapter 5, in the section on Jung.

THE CONCEPT OF TYPE

The term 'type' has connotations of mysticism, dogmatism and pigeon-holing. It is taken to be an insult and a threat to individuality. However, in Myers' theory and the MBTI, type is shorthand for 'prefers to behave in these ways and has probably developed them more, but behaves in the opposite ways too, though probably with less comfort and skill'. This expansion of the term is not mystical or dogmatic and obviously not a simple all-or-nothing pigeon-hole.

Given that 'type' is open to misunderstanding and to guilt by association with phrenology, etc., does it have any merit? I think it underlines the idea that the differences between people are profound ones, that each of us is **opposite** in some respects to people of different types. Terms like 'style', though less inflammatory, lack this quality. They sound relatively superficial.

In the MBTI, type means a difference in kind. However, the types are not intended to fit someone perfectly (which would be pigeon-holing); rather, they fit actual people to varying degrees and are intended to help in self-understanding, not to be definitive. Jung's phrase 'compass points in the wilderness of the psyche' captures this idea well.

In personality theory and research, type in this 'distinctive form' sense is generally regarded as an outmoded idea and personality characteristics are automatically treated as dimensions. Hicks (1984), Strube (1989) and York and John (1992) are among the few who have recently argued against this bias.

Some of the issues here are highly technical and statistical (see Strube and others), but the approaches to testing the value of the idea of type include:

1. Do the types behave in a qualitatively different (opposite) way from each other rather than more or less intensely? For example, in type theory, introversion is not seen as low extraversion or as the relative absence of extraversion but as the opposite quality in some respects and as existing in its own right.

2. Do people who are less clear examples of their type nevertheless behave more like clear examples of their type than like unclear examples of the opposite type? (As in (1), this expresses the crucial idea of discontinuity: is a simple division into, say, extraverts and introverts or ISTJs and ENFPs more closely related to behaviour than those characteristics measured as dimensions?) Harvey and Murray (1994) seem to show that a complex computer scoring system produces bipolar distributions of MBTI results. However, their study needs replicating and, in my view, the third sense of 'type' distinguished here is the most useful at present.

3. Does the central idea in type dynamics – that the four functions S, N, T and F can be ordered from most important to least in each type (in normal development) – have any validity? This issue is explored further in Chapter 3.

A 'TWIST' IN THE DESCRIPTIONS OF THE TYPES

The general tone of the personality descriptions in type theory is very positive. However, there is a 'twist' – that strengths tend to have corresponding weaknesses. Tables 1.4 and 1.5 illustrate this principle through aspects of two opposite types.

Table 1.4: The 'other side' of type (example 1)

ENFPs tend to be

- enthusiastic
- versatile
- lively
- insightful

But they may also:

- try to do too much
- overlook relevant details
- not finish or 'digest' projects and ideas

Table 1.5: The 'other side' of type (example 2)

ISTJs tend to be:

- thorough
- systematic
- careful with detail

But they may also:

- seem unsympathetic and inflexible
- overlook long-range implications
- expect others to conform to standard methods

The principle is discussed and applied further on pp.114–15, in the section on counsellor training.

TYPE'S MODEL OF DEVELOPMENT

Type theory includes ideas about development and change. This is a further counter to the charge of pigeon-holing. Essentially the theory states that each of us remains one type throughout life but that we develop both our true type and the 'other side'. The theory further suggests a sequence and very approximate timing for each type's development, which continues throughout life. Each type is seen as having its own natural pattern of growth. As discussed earlier, type is also optimistic about how much most people have developed their true type.

THE MBTI

This section first describes the MBTI and then briefly reviews two key aspects of any psychological measure: reliability and validity. The main chapters on validity are Chapters 2 and 3. The conditions under which people complete the MBTI are discussed in Chapter 10 and interpreting MBTI results in Chapter 2.

Technically, the MBTI (Form G) is a 95-item forced-choice paper-and-pencil questionnaire. (Items 96–126 are not scored; they are there for research purposes.) The MBTI is highly consistent with Myers' theory, though less so with Jung's (see Chapter 5). It is quite straightforward – deliberately so – and takes about 20–30 minutes to complete. Purchase is restricted to people who have completed courses in psychological testing or on the MBTI itself. Addresses of the relevant organizations are given in the Appendix. However, the theory can be very useful in its own right, without using the MBTI.

The MBTI is very widely used. In 1983, more than 750 000 copies were sold; in 1993, over 3 million (figures from Consulting Psychologists Press, the publishers). Of course, commercial success and popularity are not guarantees of high quality. A rigorous evaluation of a psychological measure focuses on its reliability and validity.

Reliability

Reliability is mainly concerned with the extent to which a measure gives the same results each time. Occasionally, when someone completes the MBTI twice the results are very different; if this happened to most people, or even a substantial minority, and there were no unusual features of the people or the conditions, then the value of the measure would be seriously threatened.

The reliability of the MBTI is affected by such factors as the age and achievement level of people completing it (Myers and McCaulley, 1985, Chapter 10). However, on average it is over 0.80, which is generally regarded as good for a personality measure. Moreover, when someone's MBTI results change, it is most likely to occur in only one of the preferences and also when the number part of the first set of results is low.

Validity

There are two main kinds of evidence for the MBTI's validity:

1. relationships with other personality measures;
2. relationships with behaviour, either of a complex kind, e.g. choosing a career, or much more simple, e.g. having a library card.

The best evidence so far for the MBTI's validity is its relationship with measures of the Big Five personality factors. Five factor theory dominates current research on personality, e.g. McAdams (1992), Goldberg (1993). Because of the close relationship between the Big Five and the preferences (see Chapter 2), research on them is in effect research on the MBTI and the extensive, high quality validity research on the Big Five supports – in a 'piggyback' way – the MBTI's validity. However, it does so at the level of four personality characteristics (see Chapter 2) and not the dynamic aspects of type theory, which are much more speculative (Chapter 3).

A further cautionary note is that validation of a personality measure is a matter of testing hypotheses, refining methods and gradually building up a picture. Each relationship and non-relationship is potentially helpful in clarifying the true meaning of each measure and the concept it is intended to represent.

HISTORY OF THE MBTI

The history of the MBTI can be summarized as Jung's observations clarified and developed by Briggs and Myers. Jung is said to have puzzled over the differences between himself and Freud, with his book *Psychological Types* (1923) as the result. Briggs, independently of Jung, was also studying personality, particularly in biographies. She too developed a type theory (Briggs, 1926). Then, when *Psychological Types* was published in America, she received it with great enthusiasm, abandoned her own similar but less formed ideas and for the next 20 years worked with her daughter, Isabel Myers, to test the theory informally. In this book I've referred to Myers' type theory because I believe she did most, particularly through the MBTI and her 1980 book *Gifts Differing*, to clarify and develop the current version of the theory, but clearly it rests on the work of Jung and Briggs too.

Myers talked about several 'pieces of tremendous luck' which led to the MBTI (Myers, 1973). The first was her early education. Her father was a research physicist who believed that the most enjoyable thing in the world was to discover something new. Myers came to believe that too. She also went to school only occasionally – her mother, Katharine Briggs, taught her and she learned to work on independent projects. Another 'piece of luck' was that Myers' husband (an ISTJ) was a very different type both from herself (INFP) and from the Briggs family. This gave Myers a 'domestic typology lab'.

Lawrence (1986) described the obstacles facing Myers and Briggs as they set out to devise a measure of psychological type. They weren't psychologists. They didn't know any statistics. In the 1940s psychological testing was new and personality tests of the questionnaire kind almost unknown. Jung was European and obscure. Moreover, Myers and Briggs had related behaviour to type for years but they didn't know whether self-report would work. They wanted to use everyday language. They weren't interested – as psychological tests generally are – in how much of a characteristic a person had, but in preference. They wanted to be able to identify the dominant function. They wanted their measure to work with people whose preferences were less well developed as well as with clearer examples of a type. And computers were not available to do the item analyses.

To give just a flavour of their item analysis: a particular item was tried out on people they knew well and who were consistently either thinking or feeling in their behaviour. If an item was answered in a thinking direction by the thinking group 60% or more of the time and in a feeling direction less than 50% of the time by the feeling group, it was kept. There are no magic items! Moreover, the item also had to **not** measure the other preferences and to work on people they didn't know and who did not have such clear preferences (at least in their behaviour).

There is much more (see Saunders' (1991) biography, Myers (1987) and Lawrence (1986)). However, I wanted to acknowledge the MBTI's extraordinary history even though this book is about its qualities, limitations and applications.

CONCLUSIONS

The MBTI has some very unusual qualities. Its positive tone makes it relatively unthreatening to complete and interpret. The theory includes a model of personality development but the MBTI doesn't measure development – which again makes it less threatening. The concept of preference is related to other concepts in major personality theories, for example 'actualization of the real self' from the humanistic approach and 'assertiveness' from the cognitive–behavioural approach. Preference is a subtle concept which allows for human qualities like self-deception, faking, feeling 'right' and fulfilment. Most people accept the idea of true preferences quite readily, saying, for example, 'Yes, I can do that but it's not really me'. The MBTI also has an unusual history, in harmony with what it tries to do.

But given all this, for me the key questions are: How valid is it? And how useful?

The validity of the MBTI: the preferences

Test results have a certain authority. The term 'Indicator' in the MBTI attempts to put this authority into a proper perspective, with MBTI results regarded as starting points rather than definitive judgements. Other personality test results are meant to be treated in this provisional way too, as sets of hypotheses which can be expanded and tested through skilful interviewing.

I have not included a 'type test' in this book because it would be too open to misuse. It is one thing to say 'These **results** say I'm an extravert with a score of 25 (which is twice as many as you)' and quite another to say 'Reading these **descriptions** I sound more like an extravert than an introvert (and you sound rather in between)'. The first has a spurious authority, which someone with skill and sensitivity should be there to prevent and if necessary challenge; the second still carries some risk but one that is accepted by codes of ethics as reasonable.

Some books on type do include a questionnaire, e.g. Keirsey and Bates (1978). Their questionnaire may be valid; no-one has yet correlated it formally with the MBTI and published the results. Moreover, the authors recommend the MBTI as more accurate than their measure (presumably from unpublished data or out of modesty). However, the ethical objection still stands.

In this chapter I do four things:

1. suggest guidelines for helping someone discover their psychological type. These express in a concrete and practical way the general principles stated above and include sections on giving feedback and on explanations for ambiguous results;
2. comment on the issue of the practical significance (as opposed to the statistical significance) of research findings;
3. describe and discuss the following sources of evidence and ideas on the validity of the MBTI and the meaning of each of the preferences:
   - research on the MBTI itself
   - research on the Big Five and other personality factors related to the MBTI

- ● ideas from the Expanded Analysis Report of the MBTI (EAR), also known as Form K of the MBTI;
4. Examine each of the eight MBTI preferences, drawing on those sources and selecting some questions which seem particularly worth studying further.

HELPING SOMEONE DISCOVER AND CHECK THEIR PSYCHOLOGICAL TYPE

Even when someone is sure about their type, it is worth encouraging them to check. I thought I was one type (INTJ) for over a year despite a close friend's clear and well-argued disagreement and she was right. Jan, an ISTJ on her initial and verified MBTI results, argued that I was not a TJ. My view was that she was a very clear TJ and that I was a less clear one but still a TJ and we left it there for over a year. This error is partly explained by my being so pleased with the I and N part of my MBTI result that I took for granted that the TJ part was accurate too. Moreover, I liked the INTJ description most and (this was long before there was a major UK interest in the MBTI) I did not have a workshop or a practitioner to help me verify my type.

Lowe (1992) discussed a similar experience. His MBTI results were INTJ too and after 'detailed feedback' from a colleague, he decided he actually was an INTJ. When he showed his wife the INTJ description, her reaction was 'That's nothing like you!'. She chose the INTP description but it was two years before Lowe finally agreed with her, as a result of feedback on the four-day MBTI Qualifying Workshop. He comments that:

> At the risk of sounding corny, it was a liberating experience ... my actions become clear to me; I understood the reasons for many of my motivations. When I looked back at the INTJ description, I wondered how on earth I could ever have thought it described me. (p. 4)

He also raises the issue of one-to-one feedback versus group feedback, seeing the former as more ethical (and expensive). I disagree. I think one of the best sources of evidence is an MBTI workshop, in which the types can be seen in action. Perceptive friends and others also appear to be good sources, if listened to seriously! (See Chapters 6 and 10.)

The following guidelines are for helping someone discover or check their type. This may mean discussing their MBTI results (part 1) or using another method for making a provisional choice of type (part 2). Some of the points in part 1 are relevant to all methods of discovering or verifying someone's type. However, the MBTI is available only to psychologists or to people who have passed a qualifying exam at the end of a four-day course (plus a substantial amount of study preparing for the course). The purpose of these restrictions is to try to prevent unethical use.

An important general principle is that any pressure to decide on your true type quickly should be resisted. Rather, you 'set the scene for the search' (Myers and McCaulley, 1985, p. 57).

Feedback of MBTI results

Ask about the person's reaction to the MBTI and their mood/state of mind when completing it (and perhaps during 'feedback' as well). Useful points may include some of the following:

- The quite large number of questions in the MBTI allows themes and patterns to emerge.
- State of mind can affect answers and it's also quite an easy questionnaire to fake, either unknowingly or deliberately. However, the results are accurate for most people.
- The MBTI measures preferences, a person's most comfortable ways of behaving (handedness, clasping hands, crossing legs are useful analogies) (See Table 1.2).
- The MBTI doesn't set out to measure intelligence or maturity.
- Most people, most of the time, behave as their preferences suggest but some-times we behave very differently. Behaviour is influenced by stress, roles, situations, other personality characteristics, motives, etc. as well as by prefer-ences (Table 1.3).
- All types are valuable in their different ways. There are no good or bad MBTI results from the viewpoint of the theory.
- Most people are quite quickly clear about their true type and usually accu-rate. It occasionally takes years to discover your type, though usually one or two of the preferences are unclear rather than all of them.
- It is not a bad thing to be unclear. Type may not apply to some people and people are much more complex than the theory.
- Individual elements within each type description may not apply to someone of that type.
- Try the format: 'People tend to be more X or more Y. Do you think either is more natural for you?'. I suggest 'outgoing' or 'reserved', 'practical' or 'interested in possibilities', 'like to analyse' or 'sympathetic', 'like to plan' or 'easygoing' as capturing central aspects of each pair of preferences.

Other methods

Methods other than the MBTI for someone to discover and to check their psychological type include:

1. careful observation of their experience and behaviour in a variety of situa-tions (ideally) or asking them about their experience and behaviour in detail.
   It may also help for the person to examine pressures on themselves, as a

child and later, to behave in particular ways. Could the pressures have led to the person not developing – or not reporting – their true type? The crucial distinction is between what feels most natural (or sometimes what the person suspects **would** feel most natural if they developed it) and what has been learned with difficulty or as a painful necessity;

2. comparing themselves with people who are probably the same type and with people who are other types. A workshop on type is the ideal setting;

3. asking people who 'know them well'. The views of close friends can be particularly helpful, as indicated earlier in this chapter;

4. reading the Report Form descriptions (in Table 3.1) or, more manageably, its definitions of the preferences.

   The person looks for the best fit rather than a perfect fit. (The descriptions are useful caricatures.) The worst fit can also be a useful clue, e.g. if a person's worst fit is ENFP, they're likely to be ISTJ. The Report Form descriptions apply best to people who have developed their dominant functions most and their auxiliaries second most, both to 'a reasonable degree'. The descriptions are still being tested and refined;

5. using temperament (SP, SJ, NT, NF) as a check on type. For example, NF *v* NT may help someone decide whether their true type is INFP or INTP;

6. using the Keirsey Temperament Sorter (probably less accurate than the MBTI, partly because it has only 70 items and partly because no information is given on how it was constructed or on its psychometric properties). Despite its name, the results are expressed as the 16 types, plus the additional possibility of a mixed type (there are 32 of these). The lowest point ethically is the statement 'You have now identified your "type"' (Keirsey and Bates, 1978, p. 12), but they add that 'the task now is to read the type description and to decide how well or how poorly the description fits' (p. 13);

7. reading longer descriptions, for example in Myers (1980), Kroeger and Thuesen (1988), Hirsh and Kummerow (1989, 1990);

8. playing the 'Insight Game', which is 36 cards with a preference statement on each side (e.g. E on one side, I on the other), giving nine cards per preference. The 1993 price was $25, from Type & Temperament Inc. (address in Appendix A);

9. completing the EAR or Form K of the MBTI (described below).

For most people, the guidelines will be sufficient for them to decide on their true type. However, two further but complex sources are the EAR (Kummerow and Quenk (1992) and this chapter) and the Personality Assessment System (Scanlon, 1990a), discussed in Chapter 4.

Giving feedback

I agree with Lord (1994) that 'The skills involved in feedback need to be given as much attention as is given to testing itself' (p. 3). Lord discussed the following potential problems in giving feedback:

1. Inter-subjectivity. Either person – the client or the person giving feedback – may interpret the same word quite differently, e.g. 'sensitive' and 'assertive'.
2. Perceived power relationships. The 'expert' may be too concerned to be accurate and right, or may be too readily seen in this way.
3. The Barnum effect. This is discussed in Chapter 5 (e.g. Table 5.1).
4. Information bias. Information bias is looking only for evidence that confirms hypotheses and ignoring evidence against.

Giving feedback is a highly skilled activity, resting on qualities like empathy and timing, as well as on a wide range of specific skills. Giving feedback on type is primarily a matter of helping the person explore their ideas and feelings about themselves. Some information-giving is also involved and the research findings on this are relatively clearcut (Bayne *et al.*, 1994). The recommendations which follow from them are for the person giving information to:

- avoid jargon
- use short words and sentences
- categorize
- vary her or his voice, and
- check understanding.

Possible explanations for ambiguous MBTI results

By 'ambiguous' I mean that the person is unsure of one or more preferences. This is most likely to happen when their number results on the MBTI are low (1–9) but it can happen with any result. In an extreme example, one person scored S35 but later decided she was an N. The possible explanations for ambiguous results include:

1. The person has completed the MBTI with an ideal in mind, e.g. ideal person, engineer, artist, manager, employee of a particular organization.
2. The person is deliberately faking.
3. The person is under great stress and temporarily 'in the grip' of their third or fourth preference.
4. The person is currently developing their third or fourth preference more than their first or second and their heightened awareness of the preference affects their answers.
5. The true preference has not been sufficiently developed: the person therefore tends to use both preferences in a pair erratically and inappropriately and in a sense is 'at war with themselves'.
6. Each of the pair of preferences is equally well developed.
7. The person believes that the type description should fit them perfectly, when it is meant to be an approximate fit.
8. The person has completed and/or scored the MBTI incorrectly.

It is not known at present which of these explanations applies most often, though (1) and (5) seem to me the most likely. Myers and McCaulley (1985, p. 58) remark that 'Low scores are more often a reflection of tension between the opposite poles of the preferences than an indication of equal excellence in both', but on the basis of experience rather than formal evidence.

PRACTICAL SIGNIFICANCE IN RESEARCH FINDINGS

Practical significance tends to be neglected in psychological research. Hudson (1968) suggested one solution, which was to calculate the proportion of observations supporting the hypothesis to those contradicting it. For example, Table 2.1 illustrates a clear relationship between judgements (after brief conversations) of the preference for judging (J) or perceiving (P) and MBTI results for J or P. Assuming the MBTI results were valid, there were 61 accurate judgements in the particular circumstances and 17 inaccurate, a proportion of better than 3:1. Thus, J and P are fairly visible in this situation but can be misjudged; there is roughly a 3:1 or 75% chance of being accurate.

Correlations are much more common in the research literature than ratios of accurate to inaccurate predictions and have been translated into 'hit rates' by Rosenthal and Rubin (1982), as indicated in Table 2.2. A correlation of 0.40 thus gives a 70% chance of being accurate and one of 0.00 a 50% or 50/50 chance. The 70% rate is of practical use and unlikely to be much higher given the number of factors influencing our experience and behaviour. Correlations of 0.40 or so are often described as 'moderate', implying 'should do better'. However, they are actually as high as can be expected: 'As the number of independent determinants of some behaviour increases, the magnitude of correlations between any one of the determinants and the behaviour must decrease' (Ahadi and Diener, 1989, p. 398).

Table 2.1: Judgements of JP related to MBTI results (from Bayne, 1988a)

MBTI

		J	P
Judgements	J	24	10
	P	7	37

Table 2.2: Correlations and 'hit rates' (based on Rosenthal and Rubin, 1982; see also Dean, 1992, and Ahadi and Diener, 1989)

Correlation	0.00	0.2	0.4	0.6
Hit rate	50% (chance: (5/10)	60% (6/10)	70% (7/10)	80% (8/10)

The finding in Table 2.1 also raises such questions as: What cues were used? In which situations are J and P less visible? Are the other preferences equally visible? Are some people better than others at judging J and P? These questions are discussed in Chapter 6, on observing type more accurately.

SOURCES OF EVIDENCE ON THE VALIDITY AND MEANING OF THE PREFERENCES

In this section, I introduce the three main sources of evidence on the MBTI's validity. Anecdotal evidence – vivid descriptions which illustrate the preferences or types and are drawn usually from the authors' own experience – is available in other books (e.g. Kroeger and Thuesen, 1988; Hirsh and Kummerow, 1989). I will draw on anecdotes only occasionally, where they seem particularly useful. They are less likely to be accurate than statements based on larger samples and give no indication of how many exceptions there are. Several sections in other chapters are also relevant to the MBTI's validity: on ratings of the accuracy of the MBTI descriptions (Chapter 5); type and occupation, conflict and stress (Chapter 9); type dynamics (Chapter 3); and research on cues to aid accurate observation (Chapter 6).

Research on the MBTI itself

The most obvious source of evidence on the MBTI's validity is research on the MBTI itself. Although this has been surprisingly sparse so far (as discussed in Chapter 5, question two), some of it has been of high quality, notably Thorne and Gough (1991).

Thorne and Gough (1991) analysed information gathered over a period of 30 years in a centre for studying personality and creativity. People of many occupations and backgrounds (but generally well-educated) and with a wide age range were observed in a variety of situations, including interviews, leaderless group discussions, role plays and mealtimes. Checklists of personality terms and other ways of describing personality were then completed by the observers independently of each other and without knowing the MBTI types (or any other personality measure results) of the people they were observing. The interviewers tended to agree with each other and Thorne and Gough report the highest correlations between (a) their descriptions and (b) MBTI preferences and types. They also report correlations with other personality measures.

Thorne and Gough's results are limited by culture and by period and some of the observations seem to reflect cultural bias against thinking females and feeling males. This applies particularly to more inferential 'observations', e.g. describing male INFJs as 'submissive' (p. 102), especially when the observations are also value-laden. Another common adjective for describing INFJs was 'unassuming', which seems to me to describe much the same behaviour but in a more positive way. Other observations are much less inferential, being more descriptions of *behaviour*, e.g. 'using hands a lot when talking'.

Other problems with the Thorne and Gough research are that the observers are described as 'well-trained' (p. 2) but few details are given, and their types and, more importantly, their competence at observing are unknown. However, there were multiple observers and observations – typically 15–18 observers studied groups of about ten people for one to three days – and both of these aspects are associated with greater accuracy (Kenrick and Funder, 1988).

Another kind of MBTI research relates type and preferences to choice of occupation. This evidence is reviewed in Chapter 9. There is also research relating type to other personality questionnaires and to various attitudes and behaviours. I have selected what seem to me the most useful of these. I think many of these studies are too poorly designed to be worth including, e.g. relating the MBTI to a questionnaire of doubtful or unknown worth or to a behaviour which is of little or no relevance or misusing the number part of MBTI scores (as discussed in Chapter 5).

The Big Five

Five factor theory currently dominates personality research. As one reviewer put it: 'After decades of doubt and defensiveness, traits are back on top' (McAdams, 1992, p. 329) and another: '... an age-old scientific problem has begun to look tractable' (Goldberg, 1992, p. 26). 'Age-old problem' and 'decades of doubt' refer to the personality versus situation debate discussed in Chapter 5.

The MBTI and the Big Five, not surprisingly, both assume that there are consistent and stable individual differences in personality and that people can describe themselves reasonably accurately if asked appropriate questions. They part company on the notion of 'type' and on some of the elements and characteristics of each personality characteristic but there is broad agreement and some of the best evidence for the validity of the MBTI comes ironically from a critique (and attempted take-over) by McCrae and Costa (1989).

As part of their programme of research to develop and test their major trait theory of personality, McCrae and Costa related their measure to the MBTI, with the results summarized in Table 2.3.

Table 2.3: Relationships between four of the Big Five factors and the MBTI in females (and males)

	Extraversion	Openness	Agreeableness	Conscientiousness
EI	0.69 (0.74)			
SN		0.69 (0.72)		
TF			0.46 (0.44)	
JP				0.46 (0.49)

Part of Table 3, McCrae and Costa (1989, p. 30), N=468, cited in Bayne (1994). Correlations all given as positive and all other correlations omitted for simplicity of presentation.

Research on five factor theory has been more vigorously pursued than research on the MBTI. Part of its high quality is that the main measure of the Big Five comes in two forms: self-report (like the MBTI) and an observer rating version. Another element is that some of the research draws on a panel of the general population. The importance of the research on five factor theory for the validity of the MBTI rests on the fact that four of the Big Five factors are closely related to the preferences (Table 2.3). Research on them is therefore in effect research on the four preferences and supports – in a 'piggyback' way – this aspect of the MBTI's validity (though not its dynamic, typological aspects).

The evidence for the validity of five factor theory is as follows: McCrae and Costa have correlated their measures with other self-report scales and psychological tests – this is routine. More importantly, they have correlated the measures with peer, spouse and clinician ratings, tested for stability of the results over several years and found that the measures predict real life outcomes like occupational change and happiness. For example, agreement between self-reports and spouse or mean peer ratings are consistently between 0.40 and 0.60 (e.g. McCrae, 1991). As Table 2.2 shows, this degree of relationship is of substantial practical value. The correlations support the validity of both self-reports and observer ratings. Expert ratings and behavioural observations, e.g. Funder and Sneed (1993), provide further support (Chapter 6).

Similarly, research on five factor theory shows that people do not change much in basic personality just because they get older – at least not in the broad characteristics identified by the theory. Correlations six years apart between self-reports and ratings by spouses range from 0.75 to 0.86 (e.g. McCrae, 1991). This very high level of stability has also been found by other researchers. It does not imply that we do not develop our personalities as we get older, more that in certain basic respects each of us is recognizably the same person, particularly from about 30 years old. Type theory assumes that where there is change before 30, it is in expression and development of type rather than type itself (Chapter 4).

McCrae and Costa (in press) argue that their model 'appears to capture the major dimensions of personality common to most personality scales' – in other words, that it is comprehensive. The Conscientiousness factor, for example, relates to needs for achievement and order, to measures of superego strength and to numerous other motives and behaviours. The factors are not narrowly behavioural but 'complex psychological structures' with cognitive, interpersonal, motivational and stylistic aspects. And their programme of research relating the five factors to other theories is intended to deepen understanding of the five as well as to reconceptualize other systems. However, the reverse can also be argued: that findings on the Big Five can be used to deepen understanding of type and the preferences (Bayne, 1994). Indeed, I would say that the relationship between the two theories (Table 2.3) is ideal for type theory: strong enough to provide good evidence for the MBTI's construct validity, but leaving room for different interpretations.

The MBTI Expanded Analysis Report

The Expanded Analysis Report (EAR) breaks each pair of preferences down into five subscales, giving 20 subscales altogether. This is a different level of analysis from the preferences and types: better for some purposes but not others. The EAR is a fairly new measure (Kummerow and Quenk, 1992) and in this book will be used in a limited way only, as a source of ideas for clarifying the meaning of the preferences. There is very little research on it so far. Its use requires specialized training beyond the MBTI Qualifying Workshop (see addresses at the end of the book) and it has two main purposes: identifying individual differences within each type and clarifying ambiguous MBTI results (Kummerow and Quenk, 1992, p. 2). Further, it does not claim to capture the whole meaning of each preference; rather, the subscales refer to 'some of the behavioural aspects' of each preference (p. 11).

At the risk of mistreating the subscales, I will treat them as bipolar descriptions of aspects of each preference and list them in a series of tables, one for each pair of MBTI preferences. This is risky in two ways. The EAR variables are treated, somewhat paradoxically, as traits rather than types – showing how much a person has of each quality – and the concepts are subtle, yet I'm presenting them in a very abbreviated form. What I want to do, though, is indicate the general range of meaning of each pair of preferences and they provide a concise contribution towards this.

THE PREFERENCES

In this section I consider each pair of preferences in turn, selecting evidence and ideas from a variety of sources, particularly those discussed above, and reaching some tentative conclusions. I will try to focus on two key aspects of each prefer-ence:

1. the behaviours and experiences which capture it best, seem most characteris-tic and in my view have the strongest empirical support;
2. what may be the underlying principle or process involved in it.

Myers, in constructing the MBTI, concentrated on the first of these, 'describ-ing the consequences (observed and inferred) rather than the processes' (1980, p. 24).

Three further introductory points. First, the terms for the preferences are used in everyday life and are open to misinterpretation. The problem is a general one in personality: Jung admitted to 'much brainracking' about it (1923, p. 538), while McCrae and Costa (1993) devote a chapter to discussing the best name for just one of their factors (the one most closely related to the SN preference). Jung went on to say of another of the preferences that 'The chief difficulty is that the word "feeling" can be used in all sorts of different ways ... but ulti-mately it is only a question of terminology. It is as if we were debating whether to call a certain animal a leopard or a panther, when all we need to know is what name we are going to give to what' (1923, p. 538). The names of the MBTI preferences are well established, but I want to acknowledge that they too cause problems. However, giving them new names would be unlikely to help. The more realistic strategy is to introduce and use them with care.

Second, the meaning of the preferences is still being clarified. They are not accurately captured in a few words. Indeed, the risk is of appearing too precise and stultifying them. And third, I have included some correlations, e.g. 0.43 between being a female E and being judged as 'outgoing' (Thorne and Gough, 1991). These are to indicate the approximate relationship and its value, as discussed earlier; where a correlation is not given (to avoid large numbers of them peppering the pages to no useful purpose) it is of the same order as those that are.

Extraversion and introversion

In type theory, extraversion (E) and introversion (I) refer to the direction in which attention and energy are most easily drawn. For Es it is outwards: 'There is a desire to act on the environment, to affirm its importance, to increase its effect' (Myers and McCaulley, 1985, p.13); 'environment' is defined as 'objects and people'. Thus E is a much broader term in type theory than 'sociable'. In marked contrast, the main interests of Is are in the inner world; while Es feel pulled into the outer world (Spoto, 1989, p.22), Is feel pushed (and pulled?) into the inner world, thus valuing peace and solitude. Table 2.4 lists some of the behaviours and attitudes associated with EI. The table, and the similar ones for SN, TF and JP, are my summary from the type literature (e.g. Myers, 1980, Lawrence, 1993), of what seem to be some of the major characteristics associated with developed EI.

Table 2.4: Some of the behaviours and attitudes associated with the EI preference (from Bayne, 1988b)

Extraversion (E)	Introversion (I)
● Prefer the 'outer world' of people and things to reflection	● Prefer reflection and the 'inner world' of action
● Active	● Prefer writing to talking
● Gain energy from others	● May enjoy social contact but need to recover from it
● Want to experience things in order to understand them	● Want to understand something before trying it
● Work by trial and error	● Persistent
● Like variety	● Like a quiet space to work in

Key characteristics of Is (compared to Es) seem to include:

1. a need to be alone more, partly to recover from social contact, action or both, partly for its own sake. As Anita Brookner (an English novelist who lives alone) said in an interview, about visits from friends: 'I'm delighted to see them and delighted to see them go';
2. a need to be more cautious, especially with new situations. This is not necessarily shyness; many Is are assertive and persistent in a quiet way but also shrink and retreat from the outside world, and can experience 'the jangled painful feeling that comes from too much happening at once' (Rowe, 1989, p.257). Jung suggested that:

   There is a whole class of [people] who, at the moment of reaction to a given situation, at first draw back a little as if with an unvoiced 'No', and only after that are able to react; and there is another class who, in the same situation, come out with an immediate reaction, apparently quite confident that their behaviour is self-evidently right. (1923, p.533);

3. thinking before speaking (an E student said 'I've always marvelled how some people appear to plan what they are going to say' – note 'appear'); it is difficult, perhaps impossible, for Es to know fully – experientially – what the world is like for Is and vice versa;
4. being interested in one's own response more than wanting to know what's going on, joining in and meeting other people.

EI has been studied more than any other personality characteristic and there are substantial differences between some of the definitions and measures. For example, Kummerow (1991) compared the MBTI definition of EI with the Strong Interest Inventory's narrower one: wanting to work *most* with people (E) or with data and ideas (I). The correlation between the two measures is about 0.40, making it easy to find people who are extraverted on one and introverted on the other. Usually, though, it is sociability (or its absence) which is emphasized in EI items. This is also true of the MBTI, so its 'face validity' is in this respect low. In contrast, its construct validity is high, e.g. Thorne and Gough (1991) found high correlations (0.60 and over) with other EI scales, as do many other researchers (Myers and McCaulley, 1985). However, I think Thorne and Gough's interpretation of EI is contaminated by those scales which tend (a) to see I as just low E, and (b) to describe I in more negative terms, e.g. inhibited, unassertive.

Of more interest in Thorne and Gough's data are the relationships between EI and observations by panels of observers (5–10 people). Extraverted males and females were described as, among other qualities, gregarious, active, cheerful, enthusiastic, energetic and talkative. The largest relationships were for 'emphasizes being with others, gregarious' (0.33 for males and 0.50 for females) and 'outgoing' (0.36 for males and 0.43 for females). Conversely, introverts were described as aloof, keeping people at a distance (the largest, 0.31 for males and 0.44 for females), reserved, inhibited and shy (pp. 50–1). These relationships provide striking confirmation of the construct validity of the EI scale.

Thorne and Gough conclude that the MBTI EI scale is a measure of sociability versus detachment (p. 71). My view is that it does more than this, perhaps because unsociable Es choose the sociability items as **less inaccurate** than the detached ones, rather than with enthusiasm. This approach works well in the USA but might not in another culture in which EI items for (say) activity might lead to greater accuracy.

Four of the five EAR subscales (Table 2.5) are self-explanatory (at least in general terms). The exception is Auditory/Visual which refers to two ways of communicating: through direct contact with others, i.e. talking, or on the other hand by reading and writing. Kummerow and Quenk suggest that 'Visual people ... don't enjoy listening closely to others; when attending a lecture, they often wonder if a paper has been written on the subject that they could just read' (p. 14).

Because the EAR dimensions are treated as traits, most people are seen as comfortable using an Auditory or Visual approach depending on the kind of information. However, I think it would be an error to infer that someone with a high score on, say, Visual cannot both listen well and enjoy it, for example in a counselling session or talking with close friends. Their difficulty might be in

Table 2.5: The five EAR subscales for EI (from Kummerow and Quenk, 1992)

Subscale	Brief expansion
Gregarious/intimate	Group *v* one-to-one
Enthusiastic/quiet	Spotlight *v* solitude
Initiator/receptor	Sociable *v* reserved
Expressive/contained	Open *v* controlled
Auditory/visual	Oral *v* writing

sustaining attention, but no-one has investigated this yet nor the similar question of how much time alone Es and Is (respectively) need. There is a little research on choice of activities (e.g. Furnham, 1981) but the basic type theory assumption about EI, that the activities which excite and energize Es are draining for Is and vice versa, has not been tested systematically.

Shy extraverts and socially skilled introverts

Jemal (1991) showed that it is straightforward to find people who can reasonably be called shy extraverts; both their friends and themselves rate them as shy and they confirm that they are Es in the MBTI sense. Cheek and Buss (1981), who investigated shyness and sociability, suggested that shy–sociable people are in a state of tension: fearful of mixing with others but also wanting to.

Jemal tested two ideas from Rowe (1989) and found that her group of six shy extraverts, compared to a group of ten non-shy extraverts, reported more serious 'bad experiences' during childhood (a possible cause of shy extraversion) but did not create groups of 'imaginary friends' (a possible effect). All the participants reported 'bad experiences' and none reported fantasy groups, but five of the six shy extraverts and only two of the ten non-shy extraverts gave more serious and personal reasons for seeing their experiences as 'bad', as judged by the raters. 'Personal' reasons included parents often arguing/fighting and parents separated/divorced, while 'less personal' included sibling rivalry and problems at school.

Shy extraverts seem worth studying further, partly because shyness is a major problem; about 25% of people say that shyness is a serious enough problem for them to do something about it (Duck, 1992, p. 55). Similarly, no-one has yet studied socially skilled introverts (Is with good development of E) but this group too seems both quite large and of interest both theoretically and in developing applications, e.g. where and how did they learn the skills?

Sensing and intuition

In type theory, sensing (S) and intuition (N) refer to two ways of gathering information. S refers to 'perceptions observable by way of the senses', N to 'perception of possibilities, meanings and relationships' (Myers and McCaulley, 1985, p. 12). People who prefer S are more likely to miss patterns and possibilities; those who prefer N are more likely to miss relevant facts and practicalities. Table 2.6 lists some of the behaviours and attitudes associated with SN.

Key characteristics of Ss (compared to Ns) seem to include:

1. attending to steps and sequence more than to overviews and the general picture. I think Ns are more likely to jump from topic to topic and to give main points first (or only) rather than leading up to them. A study of conversations between pairs of Ss (in theory, particularly dominant Ss), Ss and Ns,

Table 2.6: Some of the behaviours and attitudes associated with the SN preference (from Bayne, 1988b)

Sensing (S)	Intuition (N)
● Like facts	● See possibilities and patterns
● Realistic and practical	● Imaginative, speculative
● Observant about what is actually happening	● Like to see the overall picture
● Work steadily and step by step	● Work in bursts of energy with quiet periods in between (need inspiration)
● Enjoy owning things and making them work	● Like variety
● Patient, good with detail	● Impatient with routine

and Ns would provide evidence on this, as in Thorne's (1987) study of extraverts and introverts, discussed in Chapter 6. A related difference is the S focus on the present and the N being drawn to the future. Both accordingly tend (sometimes at great cost) to neglect the other's main interest. Both can be seen as going more readily to different aspects of the 'heart of the matter': Ss the specifics of what actually happened, Ns to its meaning;

2. working more systematically. In contrast, Ns work best in bursts and the periods between, where they seem to be doing nothing, contribute to (and perhaps result from) the bursts;

3. being creative in a practical and adapting way more than a generating and novel one. Ss tend to adapt the present system; Ns prefer to start afresh, design a new and radically different way (and to dislike standard approaches). A general theme in type theory – that neither preference is better – applies here. Sometimes a sensing approach is most effective, other times an intuitive approach. Ideally, the strengths of both S and N combine rather than grate and antagonize (see pp. 141–3 in Chapter 9).

SN has the clearest relationships of any of the preferences with choice of occupation (Myers and McCaulley, 1985). Thorne and Gough (1991) found that Ns tended to be rated as 'thinking and associating to ideas in unusual ways; has unconventional thought processes' (the largest relationship; 0.36 for males, 0.40 for females), 'unpredictable and changeable in behaviour and attitudes', 'tends to be rebellious and unconforming', imaginative, ingenious, original (0.37 for males, 0.27 for females) and rebellious (pp. 51–2).

Ss were described as 'favours conservative values in a variety of areas' (0.39 for males and 0.42 for females), 'uncomfortable with uncertainty and complexities', conventional (0.38 for males and 0.45 for females), conservative, contented, practical and 'interests narrow'. Thorne and Gough comment that 'These findings agree well with MBTI lore, which views Sensing types as down-to-earth, conforming, fact-respecting and self-controlled' (p. 53); however, they agree rather less well with the SP temperament discussed in the next chapter.

Carlson (1980) asked her subjects to write a letter to an imaginary person abroad introducing themselves. She scored the letters for 'concrete self-description' and 'imaginative participation', by which she meant references to the life of the imaginary recipient of the letter. (This might have been predicted to relate to F as well as N, because of the central role of empathy in F, but 'empathy' with someone unreal is a contradiction in terms.) Ss used concrete self-descriptions more often and Ns were more 'imaginative'.

The EAR subscales of SN are listed in Table 2.7.

Table 2.7: The five EAR subscales for SN (from Kummerow and Quenk, 1992)

Subscale	Brief expansion
Concrete/abstract	Literal *v* symbolic
Realistic/imaginative	Sensible *v* ingenious
Pragmatic/intellectual	Practical *v* scholarly
Experiential/theoretical	Realistic *v* big picture
Traditional/original	Conventional *v* idiosyncratic

'Openness to experience' (the counterpart of SN) is regarded as the most controversial of the Big Five (McCrae, 1993–4) and often confused with other concepts. The suggested underlying motive is to explore and enlarge experience, hence the search for novelty. The content of the SN scale items contrasts preference for the simple and conventional with preference for the complex and original but, like the EI scale, it measures a more complex underlying characteristic.

The five factor conception of openness to experience emphasizes sensory acuity and here there is a direct clash with type theory: in five factor theory, it is high 'open to experience' people (i.e. Ns) who are most open to the senses (McCrae, 1993–4), while in type theory this is a characteristic of Ss. Thus one ISFP described descriptions of Ss by Ns as 'pale and plodding', because Ns do not (and perhaps cannot) appreciate the S quality of being in the present and really listening, etc.

The direct evidence for the five factor view is slender; it consists of one study (Kaplan and Singer, 1963) which measured sensory acuity in five modalities – smell, taste, touch, hearing and sight – and related them to a measure of dogmatism (one of the many personality measures related to 'openness to experience' and therefore to SN). Kaplan and Singer found a very high correlation, especially as there were only 26 subjects, of 0.60 between acuity and low dogmatism (and therefore to N more than S) and concluded that 'openness to sense impressions apparently runs parallel to openness to ideas' (p. 48). I find it surprising that no replications of this impressive finding have been reported.

Apart from being a test of directly competing predictions from two major theories of personality, it is potentially useful as an objective measure of a key variable.

A related aspect of SN worth investigating is its relationships with what people read and how they read. Is S preference (at least according to type theory) for 'real things' reflected in a taste for biography and thrillers rather than books of ideas or fantasy? And do Ss remember plots and names of characters better than Ns do? (TF might also be relevant here.) Nolan and Patterson (1990) found that Ss preferred the following kinds of TV programme, action, sport, situation comedy and game shows, but that Ns didn't express a preference. Nolan and Patterson (p. 705) speculated that Ss may enjoy TV more as a medium because it's a very 'immediate' activity and, in McLuhan's (1964) term, a 'cool' medium that 'tends to amputate the imagination of the viewer' (!). In contrast, books are a 'hot' medium. Unfortunately, Nolan and Patterson do not report their results straightforwardly, e.g. in terms of correlations, percentages of viewers or hours, so the strength of their findings cannot be discussed. Motives for watching particular programmes, as well as watching itself, seem worth investigating.

Hammer (1985) discussed the idea that words, because they are symbols, are less real and therefore less attractive to Ss. He asked 128 people to list the titles of 'all books they had read for pleasure in the last month' (with the word 'pleasure' in capitals), films they had seen and hours of TV they watched per day. Most of the participants had some knowledge of type theory. Ss and Ns did not differ significantly in the amount of fiction or non-fiction that they reported reading or the films and TV they had watched. Ss reported an average of 3.4 books per month and Ns 4.3. This finding conflicts with Hicks' (1984) research which found a clear difference between Ss and Ns in a group similar in age, education and proportions of each sex to Hammer's participants. Hammer discusses a number of explanations, e.g. that there are different classes of words: some represent and evoke concrete images, others are abstract symbols. Thus broad variables like 'reading' and 'reading fiction' may need to be broken down. Other kinds of variable, like styles and motives, may also need to be studied to find reliable type differences.

Would you expect sensing types to be particularly good at proof-reading (focus on immediate reality, attention to detail, etc.)? There is wide variation in this ability, with an average error detection rate of only 60–75% (West in Gordy and Thorne, 1994). Gordy and Thorne analysed data on different kinds of proof-reading errors made by 195 students. There was an excellent variety of types, at least on clear MBTI results. They were given three minutes to proof-read a passage 1¼ pages long from a popular magazine. The passage included 49 deliberately created errors. The main and counterintuitive finding was that Ns found significantly more errors (though only two more on average) than Ss. This may not have happened if the participants had been less pressured.

Gordy and Thorne also suggest that Ns are more comfortable with symbols and reading and that they may use the more efficient holistic search strategy rather than an analytic one (type theory would certainly predict this). In the holistic strategy the whole word is judged; in the analytic strategy it is the first few letters of each word. Each of these ideas would, as Gordy and Thorne point out, be easy to test. Unfortunately they did not analyse their data by type and temperament. Perhaps the most obvious group to investigate would be very competent professional proof-readers.

Thinking and feeling

Thinking (T) and feeling (F) are two ways of making decisions or coming to conclusions. They are the two terms in type theory most open to misinterpretation, as 'not having emotions' and 'not able to be logical' respectively. Neither is true. First, it is a general human characteristic to have emotions. Second, the ability to think depends on academic intelligence, a quality only slightly related to type and then to SN rather than TF. Thinking, in its MBTI sense, 'relies on principles of cause and effect and tends to be impersonal', while feeling is 'decision-making by weighing relative values' (Myers and McCaulley, 1985, p.12). Some of the qualities associated with T and F are listed in Table 2.8. The distinction between principles and values is made in the type literature but may be a semantic rather than a real difference – though the words themselves may mean more to people of each preference. I suspect that having values/principles is another general human characteristic and that the TF difference is about how values/principles are used and which takes priority.

In five factor theory, 'Agreeable' is the term for the factor corresponding (approximately) to TF. Agreeable is used in the sense of 'pleasant' and 'gentle' rather than 'conforming'. Low scorers on Agreeableness are described in terms which contrast with the MBTI's terms for T: ruthless, suspicious, uncooperative, etc. but in my view these are only extreme versions of the tough-minded, objective elements of T – or, perhaps more precisely, the relative absence of F. If most people have developed both T and F to some extent, then the less

Table 2.8: Some of the behaviours and attitudes associated with the TF preference (from Bayne, 1988b)

Thinking (T)	Feeling (F)
● Fair, firm-minded, sceptical	● Warm, sympathetic, aware of how
● Analytical and logical	others feel
● Brief and businesslike	● Trusting
● Critical	● Enjoy pleasing others
● Clear and consistent principles	● Need harmony
	● Clear and consistent values

extreme versions of the terms will be more applicable. Similarly, Fs who haven't developed sufficient T will tend to be too agreeable.

Key characteristics of Ts (compared to Fs) include:

1. an emphasis on objective criteria. Is it true or false? Is it more efficient? Fs tend to emphasize subjective criteria. Do I like or dislike it? What effect will it have on others? Does it matter to me? Am I comfortable with this? Does it feel right? Because Fs emphasize the personal and subjective, they tend to value harmony in their relationships with people and to need to appreciate and be appreciated. The idea that (crudely) some people are motivated best by praise and others by criticism may be most applicable to Fs and Ts respectively, perhaps with EI playing a part too;
2. a different attitude towards ideas and emotions. In type theory, Fs tend to be more interested in emotions than Ts, who tend to be more interested in ideas, thoughts and reasons. As one INTP put it: 'I try not to act according to feelings unless there is a rational explanation for them';
3. enjoying debates and 'getting one's teeth' into something rather than communicating enthusiasm about something that matters. T is quite a detached and logical process by definition; F, also by definition, means evaluating and therefore not being detached.

Kroeger and Thuesen (1988) illustrate part of TF with the following situation. Imagine you've agreed to lend your car to your adolescent child to go on a date that night. Meanwhile the weather has changed drastically to freezing rain. How do you decide what to do? What factors do you take into account? Table 2.9 gives some contrasting answers.

Table 2.9: Thinking and feeling: an example (based on Kroeger and Thuesen, 1988)

Thinking parent for:
Feels scared, anxious.
'Chris needs to learn to drive in bad weather sometime, so ...'

Feeling parent for:
Feels scared, anxious.
'How would I feel with a relationship at stake – I'd feel untrusted and controlled and very small, so ...'

Thinking parent against:
'Parents have to make tough decisions. Being liked is secondary ...'

Feeling parent against:
'I remember being that age and not getting the car. Next morning I realized my parents cared a lot to go through all that ...'

In good type development, both T and F are used as appropriate but with the true preference given priority. Thus Ts may 'factor in' people's feelings and viewpoints as part of the analysis which leads to a decision and Fs may examine costs and benefits as part of 'weighing' and feeling their way to a decision. Both can also use their less preferred function to make a better decision in appropriate circumstances or to get through an impasse, e.g. Fs may get stuck when two powerful values clash, Ts when they keep analysing and analysing and cannot make a decision. There are limits to both logic and values.

Thorne and Gough (1991) found that TF was less straightforward in the eyes of their observers than the other preferences; males and females were rated differently more often and the relationships were lower. Value judgements, stemming from gender stereotypes (the data were collected many years before their analysis), seem to intrude. Despite this problem, there are some useful relationships. The largest correlation for male Fs (of 0.23) was 'enjoys aesthetic impressions; is aesthetically responsive' and for females (0.35) 'has warmth; has the capacity for close relationships'. 'Affectionate' and 'sentimental' described both sexes, 'artistic' and 'sensitive' the males (both about 0.20), 'affectionate' and 'trusting' the females (both about 0.30). Ts of both sexes were described as 'prides self on being objective, rational' (0.34 for males, 0.31 for females) and 'ambitious'. Females were also described as 'hard-headed' (0.31), 'conceited, opinionated and condescending'(!) (pp. 54–5). As Thorne and Gough remark, T seems to be 'more appropriate for and acceptable in men than in women' (p. 55). They **are** a little grudging about this aspect of their data:

> There may be an element of cultural conventionality on the part of observers, who view the logical analytic style as role-appropriate for men but inappropriate for women. It may also be the case that cultural biases, as well as other factors, can lead to genuine internal and behaviour problems for women who prefer the thinking mode. (p. 74)

The possibility of genuine problems arising for female Ts and male Fs is discussed in the next section.

The EAR subscales for TF are summarized in Table 2.10. The subscale 'critical/accepting' is seen as two different ways of trying to be helpful: either focusing on things that are wrong or focusing on positive things.

Table 2.10: The five EAR subscales for TF (from Kummerow and Quenk, 1992)

Subscale	Brief expansion
Critical/accepting	Sceptical *v* tolerant
Tough/tender	Tough-minded *v* gentle
Questioning/accommodating	Independent-minded *v* like harmony
Logical/affective	Analytic *v* rely on values
Reasonable/compassionate	Just *v* sympathetic

Thinking females and feeling males

In this section I will focus on three questions about gender and type:

1. How large are gender differences in type?
2. What is conjectured about the impact of cultural expectations about gender on female thinking types and male feeling types as well as on female feeling types and male thinking types?
3. What helpful factors have been suggested to counter any adverse impacts, in either a preventive or a remedial way?

Sex differences in type

Psychological differences between the sexes are very slight (Nicholson, 1993); indeed, the overlap is so great they are more accurately called similarities. By far the largest psychological sex difference reported so far is on the TF preference; in Myers' USA general population sample (or the closest to one we have so far, data collected 1978–82), about 30% of women reported T and about 40% of men reported F. Thus there seems to be a majority of each gender whose preference for T or F is consistent with gender stereotypes, but also large minorities whose preferences go against those stereotypes. However, these are MBTI rather than verified types and the sample were 17 year olds, when sexual identity is a greater concern than for other age groups. Thus as a group they may have been more likely than adults to report in line with cultural expectation rather than with their true types.

The MBTI results of a group of 496 UK men (see Table 3.4), predominantly manual workers, collected in groups of about 20 and in three-hour workshops by Carole Martin and myself, were about 33% feeling. Given the likely pressures in these groups to report in line with male stereotypes (especially as the MBTI was completed during the workshop), this seems to me a strikingly high figure. The true proportion of thinking women and feeling men may be much closer to 50% than 30% or 40%.

Other research supports this speculation. Kummerow (1988) found that far more people changed their view of themselves from T to F after a systematic verification procedure than any of the other possible changes. However, her participants were retail and bank managers (either in a management development programme or on a training course on communication and relationships) and predominantly T. As Kummerow points out, it would be interesting to repeat the study with participants who are predominantly F and to see what happens to Ts in such a group.

Oxford Psychologists Press (1993) reported data on change between MBTI or 'Reported Type' and 'True Type' in their qualifying workshops. As in Kummerow's study – but this time with a group whose MBTI types were evenly distributed on TF – the largest number of shifts was from T to F, especially in men. About 20% of the 182 men changed from T to F and about 3%

from F to T. Results for women were more even: about 9% of the 188 women changed from T to F and about 6% from F to T.

A further factor in favour of the possibility that feeling males are reporting T is that it is currently recommended (*Bulletin of Psychological Type* (1994), **17**(1), 28) that the female TF scoring key be used for males as well as females. The UK results in Table 3.4 were collected in 1991–2 and so were scored with the male TF key.

Possible impact of cultural expectations on all combinations of TF and gender

This section is based largely on anecdote and theory (particularly from Scanlon (1989) and Stokes, (1987a,b). There is little published research on gender and type yet. No-one knows how true or how general the following ideas are or whose viewpoint they represent, e.g. do T females see other T females as aggressive and hard?

Thinking women
- Seen as aggressive and hard.
- Not popular with peers of opposite sex as young adolescents (Scanlon, 1989). Most of the INTPs in Barger and Kirby's (1993) research did not have a 'best friend' of either sex.
- May 'cover up' (be 'ladylike' and polite). This may be more likely in ISTJs than the more independent NTs and SPs (Stokes, 1987a). Stokes also suggests a 'breathy softness' of speech which tends to seem false and that 'extreme colouration' – behaving like a type other than one's own (see Chapter 4) – is the most frequent impact in USA culture. Colouration is predicted by type theory to be very draining of energy and, according to several theories of personality, could well lead to loss of sense of self.
- Feel 'different' in the sense of not fitting in (Barger and Kirby, 1993).

Feeling men
Feeling men may provide a rare example of greater oppression for males than females, because parents tend to be more concerned about the masculinity of their sons than the femininity of their daughters (Nicholson, 1993). Possible impacts include:

- accused of being wimps;
- have more female friends as adolescents (both T and F?);
- defending people who are picked on (despite a dislike of conflict).

Feeling women
Stokes (personal communication) studied a group of ENFJ women who said they wanted to be supportive but were expected to be *too* supportive and felt stressed as a result.

Thinking men

If there is a sex difference on thinking, the research about men in general applies most to this group. One characteristic of men is dying younger (Nicholson, 1993), though the substantial gap (currently of about seven years) is apparently narrowing.

Helpful factors

There are some specific possibilities here which seem worth investigating, e.g. explaining to thinking types that others may find criticism hard to take because of their pride and that helping them 'save face' might be a useful skill, and that feeling men might choose roles and occupations like priest, clown, athlete and actor (Scanlon, 1989). In general terms, the helpful factor will be anything that makes type development more likely and which takes account of the variety of roles all individuals are expected to play.

Judging and perceiving

Js tend to be visibly concerned most with 'making decisions, seeking closure, planning operations or organizing activities', while Ps are more 'attuned to incoming information' (Myers and McCaulley, 1985, p. 14). Behaviours and attitudes associated with J and P are listed in Table 2.11.

Table 2.11: Some of the behaviours and attitudes associated with the JP preference (from Bayne, 1988b)

Judging (J)	Perceiving (P)
● Decisive	● Curious
● Industrious and determined	● Flexible and tolerant
● Organized and systematic	● Leave things open
● Take deadlines seriously	● Pull things together well at last minute
● Like to have things decided and settled	● Sample many more experiences than can be digested or used

Key characteristics of Js (compared to Ps) include:

1. Js seem to try to control time by organizing it and filling it up (and may therefore find it difficult to relax). In contrast, Ps have a more easygoing approach (and may therefore find it difficult to finish things);
2. Js tend to experience imminent deadlines as a threat and a block, while Ps tend to be energized and inspired by them (and therefore to seek them out and deliberately use them).

Thorne and Gough (1991) found that Js were rated by their observers as 'favours conservative values in a variety of areas' (0.35 for males and 0.32 for females) and moralistic. Female Js were described as 'tends towards over-control of needs and impulses; binds tensions excessively; delays gratifications unnecessarily' (0.33). Both sexes were rated as conservative (0.36 for males, 0.37 for females), conventional, deliberate, industrious and methodical.

Ps were described as 'unpredictable and changeable in behaviour and attitudes' (0.34 for females), 'enjoys sensuous experiences' and 'tends to be rebellious and non-conforming' (0.40 for males). Both sexes were described as careless (0.25 for females), changeable and rebellious (0.34 for males) (pp. 55–7 and Appendices D and E).

Again, the MBTI descriptions are strongly supported. And on the EAR, the subscales for JP (Table 2.12) are similarly consistent; JP seems to be a relatively straightforward construct. In Big Five terms, though, it has a positive end and a critical one, with Js described as organized and Ps (in the form of low Conscientiousness) as aimless, lazy and disorganized. My view is that flexibility taken to an extreme and without some balance from the opposite does indeed become aimless but that organization can equally become rigid and obsessive.

Table 2.12: The five EAR subscales for JP (from Kummerow and Quenk, 1992)

Subscale	Brief expansion
Stress avoider/poly-active	Start early *v* enjoy pressure
Systematic/casual	Structured *v* easygoing
Scheduled/spontaneous	Routine *v* flexibility
Planful/open-ended	Like or dislike for long-term plans
Methodical/emergent	Organized (e.g. subtasks) *v* ad hoc

JP has not been investigated as much as the other preferences. One notable study of its parallel in five factor theory is of particular interest, though, both for one of its findings and for the variety of explanations of the finding. Friedman *et al.* (1993) found that people high on Conscientiousness (i.e. Js) live longer. Moreover, the finding was a very clear one and the effect comparable in strength to high blood pressure, though less influential than gender or smoking a packet of cigarettes a day if you are a 50 year old male (Friedman *et al.*, 1993, p. 181).

Length of life is easy to measure and, as the authors remark, 'of obvious importance'. It is less easy to study personality factors related to it and the data were taken from a study begun in 1921 on 856 males and 672 females who were born between 1904 and 1915. The measures of personality were ratings by a parent and a teacher.

Interpreting the relationship between J and longevity is difficult. Knowing cause of death might help and this is being studied. Friedman *et al.* suggest that Conscientious people:

- tend to take better care of their health;
- take fewer risks;
- cooperate more with medical treatment;
- prepare better and thus reduce stress; and/or
- cope more effectively with stress.

A further complexity (more cheerful for Ps?) is that the group of people studied grew up in a simpler, more structured time than the 1990s: 'We should not be too quick to generalize these findings to today's children, who are facing some different threats to their health' (p. 184). This does not make the research pointless. The logic of science is often to find a relationship (e.g. mould and healing) and then focus more precisely on the mechanisms (e.g. penicillin), a more precise understanding of the link between longevity and JP could have implications for health education and policy (Friedman *et al.*, 1993).

In the MBTI, the JP preference is also used to point to the dominant and auxiliary functions, at the heart of the type part of type theory and the main subject of the next chapter.

CONCLUSIONS

This chapter discussed the process of helping someone discover their true type, some of the evidence for the validity of each of the preferences and the nature (as so far understood) of the preferences themselves. They are complicated. For example, Myers remarked that the social life of ESTJs and ENTJs tends to be 'incidental' and Kopp (1974) gave the example of commonly held views of Es as 'successful outgoing realists' and Is as 'peculiarly awkward bookworms' and commented that 'these notions are perhaps most dangerous not because they are wholly false but rather because they just miss the mark' (p. 109). This chapter was an attempt to bring together some of the most useful ideas and evidence on what is true and central about each of the preferences, drawing primarily on observational research, the EAR and five factor theory.

3 | The validity of the MBTI: the types and the temperaments

Portraits of Type (Thorne and Gough, 1991) is mainly packed with data but there is a warm moment in the introduction. Thorne relates how, as a first year graduate student, she 'mustered the courage' to ask her professor 'Do introverted thinkers *really* behave differently than introverted feelers?' and he replied 'What type are you?' as if his own question were relevant and the answer really mattered (p.xiii). This chapter is concerned with both questions and with a variety of answers to them at levels beyond those discussed in Chapter 2. The evidence discussed in Chapter 2 showed clearly that in one sense of type, introverted thinkers and introverted feelers do indeed behave differently, if only because of the TF difference. But Thorne's question has a deeper meaning. In a more precise form, it can be expressed as: 'Are introverted thinkers and feelers different in other ways than can be attributed to thinking and feeling alone?'.

When they are part of a type theory rather than four independent major personality characteristics, the preferences are divided into attitudes (EI and JP) and functions (SN and TF). The attitudes and functions interact with each other in this meaning of type, which is called 'type dynamics'. In particular, the key idea is that in each type one of the four functions usually dominates the others. Of the three meanings of the term 'type' touched on in Chapter 1, this seems to me the most crucial and the most directly related to concepts like 'being one's real self'. Myers' type theory assumes that if someone does not express their dominant function sufficiently and more than any of the other functions they are unlikely to feel fulfilled or at their best.

This chapter is in five parts, concerned with:

1. an overview of the various descriptions of the types available in the literature and what is known about how many people of each type there are;
2. type dynamics, particularly the concept of the dominant function;
3. the evidence on the validity of the MBTI types, both in terms of behaving

differently from the other types and, more specifically, behaving as indicated by the respective dominant functions;
4. the radically simpler approach of Keirsey's temperament theory, which bypasses type dynamics and complexities like the difference between preference and behaviour and suggests that distinguishing between just four patterns of behaviour is practical and powerful;
5. other combinations of the preferences than those in temperament theory.

DESCRIPTIONS OF THE TYPES

The descriptions of the types seen first by most people are in the standard Report Form (Table 3.1). These descriptions are deliberately brief and can be compared to cartoons: they try to pick out only the most characteristic and recognizable aspects of each type. Their purpose, of course, is to help people decide on their own type and then move on to more detailed descriptions. Generally they are effective (relevant research is discussed in Chapter 5).

If you wish to employ Table 3.1 in this way, two main strategies can be used. The first is obvious. If you are sure about one preference, then that reduces your possible true types to eight, so compare those eight for 'best fit' (i.e. not perfect fit). If you are sure about two preferences, then there are only four types which could be your true type – assuming you are accurate about the two preferences. The second strategy is a check on the first: look for the 'worst fit', the description least like you, as a clue to the best fit. For both strategies please bear in mind the guidelines at the beginning of Chapter 2 and be open to new evidence, e.g. the views of anyone who knows you well and more detailed descriptions than those in Table 3.1.

There are many good sources of more detailed descriptions. For example, Hirsh and Kummerow (1989) wrote a chapter on each type, with each chapter structured around seven themes plus a summary: living, learning, labouring, leading, leisure, loving, losing out and 'in a nutshell'. Kroeger and Thuesen (1988, 1992, 1994) describe each type in general terms in three or four pages (1988), at work in five to seven pages (1992) and in loving relationships in two or three pages (1994). Keirsey and Bates (1978) give general descriptions of about two pages per type in an appendix. All these books and those in the next paragraph also describe each of the preferences in its own right and sometimes various combinations as well.

Hirsh and Kummerow (1990), in a more businesslike context, describe each type in one page, bullet-point style: contributions to the organization, leadership style, potential pitfalls, preferred work environment and suggestions for development. And Hammer (1993) is similarly concise and systematic: again one page per type, but this time with the focus on careers and career development.

Myers' (1976) early descriptions of the types – in *Introduction to Type* – embodied an ingenious idea: she wrote them in different styles to try to communicate best with the type she was describing. For example, the Thinking descriptions

Table 3.1: The Report Form descriptions. Characteristics frequently associated with each type

	Sensing Types		Intuitive Types	
ISTJ Serious, quiet, earn success by concentration and thoroughness. Practical, orderly, matter-of-fact, logical, realistic and dependable. See to it that everything is well organized. Take responsibility. Make up their own minds as to what should be accomplished and work toward it steadily, regardless of protests or distractions.		**ISFJ** Quiet, friendly, responsible and conscientious. Work devotedly to meet their obligations. Lend stability to any project or group. Thorough, painstaking, accurate. Their interests are usually not technical. Can be patient with necessary details. Loyal, considerate, perceptive, concerned with how other people feel.	**INFJ** Succeed by perseverance, originality and desire to do whatever is needed or wanted. Put their best efforts into their work. Quietly forceful, conscientious, concerned for others. Respected for their firm principles. Likely to be honored and followed for their clear convictions as to how best to serve the common good.	**INTJ** Usually have original minds and great drive for their own ideas and purposes. In fields that appeal to them, they have a fine power to organize a job and carry it through with or without help. Skeptical, critical, independent, determined, sometimes stubborn. Must learn to yield less important points in order to win the most important.
ISTP Cool onlookers – quiet, reserved, observing and analyzing life with detached curiosity and unexpected flashes of original humor. Usually interested in cause and effect, how and why mechanical things work, and in organizing facts using logical principles.		**ISFP** Retiring, quietly friendly, sensitive, kind, modest about their abilities. Shun disagreements, do not force their opinions or values on others. Usually do not care to lead but are often loyal followers. Often relaxed about getting things done, because they enjoy the present moment and do not want to spoil it by undue haste or exertion.	**INFP** Full of enthusiasms and loyalties, but seldom talk of these until they know you well. Care about learning, ideas, language and independent projects of their own. Tend to undertake too much, then somehow get it done. Friendly, but often too absorbed in what they are doing to be sociable. Little concerned with possessions or physical surroundings.	**INTP** Quiet and reserved. Especially enjoy theoretical or scientific pursuits. Like solving problems with logic and analysis. Usually interested mainly in ideas, with little liking for parties or small talk. Tend to have sharply defined interests. Need careers where some strong interest can be used and useful.

ESTP	ESFP	ENFP	ENTP
Good at on-the-spot problem solving. Do not worry, enjoy whatever comes along. Tend to like mechanical things and sports, with friends on the side. Adaptable, tolerant, generally conservative in values. Dislike long explanations. Are best with real things that can be worked, handled, taken apart or put together.	Outgoing, easygoing, accepting, friendly, enjoy everything and make things more fun for others by their enjoyment. Like sports and making things happen. Know what's going on and join in eagerly. Find remembering facts easier than mastering theories. Are best in situations that need sound common sense and practical ability with people as well as with things.	Warmly enthusiastic, high-spirited, ingenious, imaginative. Able to do almost anything that interests them. Quick with a solution for any difficulty and ready to help anyone with a problem. Often rely on their ability to improvise instead of preparing in advance. Can usually find compelling reasons for whatever they want.	Quick, ingenious, good at many things. Stimulating company, alert and outspoken. May argue for fun on either side of a question. Resourceful in solving new and challenging problems, but may neglect routine assignments. Apt to turn to one new interest after another. Skillful in finding logical reasons for what they want.
ESTJ	**ESFJ**	**ENFJ**	**ENTJ**
Practical, realistic, matter-of-fact, with a natural head for business or mechanics. Not interested in subjects they see no use for, but can apply themselves when necessary. Like to organize and run activities. May make good administrators, especially if they remember to consider others' feelings and points of view.	Warm-hearted, talkative, popular, conscientious, born cooperators, active committee members. Need harmony and may be good at creating it. Always doing something nice for someone. Work best with encouragement and praise. Main interest is in things that directly and visibly affect people's lives.	Responsive and responsible. Generally feel real concern for what others think or want and try to handle things with due regard for the other person's feelings. Can present a proposal or lead a group discussion with ease and tact. Sociable, popular, sympathetic. Responsive to praise and criticism.	Hearty, frank, decisive, leaders in activities. Usually good in anything that requires reasoning and intelligent talk, such as public speaking. Are usually well informed and enjoy adding to their fund of knowledge. May sometimes appear more positive and confident than their experience in an area warrants.

were more analytical. As far as I know, no-one tested their effectiveness and in the current, fifth edition (1993), the descriptions have become more detailed but also uniform in style, with the following subsections: At their best, Characteristics, How others may see them, Potential areas for growth. Finally, Brownsword (1987) too describes the types in general terms, one or two pages each, as part of a book which has the relationship between type and temperament as a main theme.

Three things stand out for me in these descriptions. First, people generally recognize their type, sometimes with delight, sometimes ruefully. Second, the emphasis is on positive qualities but it is not only positive, e.g. the sections on potential pitfalls and areas to develop in Hirsh and Kummerow (1990). Third, they are generally based on extensive experience rather than on empirical research. As I read them, I think 'Yes, that's well put and true of X and Y' or 'That doesn't sound right – it's over-stated' or 'too general' or 'wrong'. And I expect other people do the same, to varying degrees, but reacting to *different* elements. The descriptions are thus something of a 'lucky dip' at the moment, though with substantial overlap, and we need to compare them and to test their validity, both perceived validity (as discussed in Chapter 5, criticism four) and relationships with behaviour. Type theory suggests that different descriptions would be most meaningful to different types. However, I think type is concerned with general aspects and that – like writing different descriptions for women and men of each type – it would be a loss and to some extent self-defeating to become more specific. At the same time I recognize that if, say, INTP women and men really are substantially and sufficiently different, then that loss will be necessary.

Incidence of the types

Table 3.2 shows the best estimate so far of the incidence of MBTI types in the USA general population. Thus on this evidence ESTJ and ESFJ occur the most frequently and INFJ and INTJ the least. This is because in the USA there seem to be three extraverts to every introvert and three people who prefer sensing to every person who prefers intuition. TF and JP appear to be more equally distrib- uted but with a gender difference on TF (as discussed in Chapter 2) and there are about 55% Js to 45% Ps (McCaulley *et al.*, 1985).

There are problems with Tables 3.2 and 3.3. The MBTI results are from a large sample of high school students (about 17 or 18 years old), but some types may be more likely to drop out of school and some less likely to complete a measure like the MBTI or to complete it with interest or honesty. A limitation of a different kind is that there may be cultural differences in the frequency of the types. Table 3.4 gives the MBTI types of a UK sample of men employed in a large public sector organization. It seems that introverts may be more frequent than extraverts in the UK but that the 3:1 S to N ratio may be about the same as in the USA. The least common male types are again INTJ and INFJ.

Table 3.2: Proportions (%) of MBTI types in the USA general population (my calculations from Tables 4.12 and 4.13 of Myers and McCaulley, 1985)

ISTJ 7	ISFJ 7	INFJ 2	INTJ 3
ISTP 4	ISFP 5	INFP 4	INTP 4
ESTP 7	ESFP 10	ENFP 8	ENTP 5
ESTJ 15	ESFJ 14	ENFJ 4	ENTJ 4

SP 23%   SJ 43%   NT 16%   NF 18%   N = 9,500

Table 3.3: Proportions (%) of male and female types in the USA general population (from Myers and McCaulley, 1985; my calculations of the percentages, rounding up)

ISTJ M 9 F 5	**ISFJ** M 5 F 10	**INFJ** M 2 F 2	**INTJ** M 4 F 2
ISTP M 6 F 2	**ISFP** M 5 F 6	**INFP** M 4 F 5	**INTP** M 5 F 2
ESTP M 9 F 4	**ESFP** M 7 F 12	**ENFP** M 6 F 10	**ENTP** M 7 F 3
ESTJ M 17 F 13	**ESFJ** M 8 F 21	**ENFJ** M 3 F 5	**ENTJ** M 6 F 3

Table 3.4: Proportions (%) of male MBTI types in a large UK organization (data collected by Carole Martin and myself, 1991–2, in workshops of about 20, total N = 496)

ISTJ	ISFJ	INFJ	INTJ
23	10	1	0
ISTP	ISFP	INFP	INTP
11	8	2	3
ESTP	ESFP	ENFP	ENTP
8	6	2	3
ESTJ	ESFJ	ENFJ	ENTJ
16	4	1	2

Despite their limitations, tables of MBTI types provide good evidence for the types being different in their choice of occupation. Chapter 9 includes examples of type distributions in business, psychology and counselling students, for example, and Myers and McCaulley (1985) include data on each of the types which show distinctive patterns of most and least chosen careers, despite the many other factors – luck, advice, fashion, availability – involved in choice of career.

Two areas for further research here are to study type, competence and job satisfaction and how people who are in unusual jobs for their type cope. (Some jobs are much more open to individual styles than others, of course.) For example, which aspects of psychology – a very diverse subject but predominantly intuitive – are sensing psychology students drawn to most and least and how do they respond to the majority intuitive lecturers and peers? I think psychology needs more sensing types – by definition, we lack their strengths at the moment – to become more balanced and applied. We know that in the USA sensing types are found more frequently in experimental psychology (about 34%) and less in clinical (about 5%) (Myers and McCaulley, 1985).

Nearly all the research on the MBTI has been on one or other of the preferences. The obvious reason for this is the large number of participants needed to study all the types, e.g. ten persons per type is 160 participants, not allowing for age, gender, educational background, etc. However, this does not explain why there are so few studies of temperament or other combinations or of one or two types in depth. Carlson and Levy (1973) are an exception. They very straight-forwardly predicted, as part of their study, that the types most attracted to voluntary overseas work would be ENTPs and ENFPs and found that this was true for seven of ten volunteers. It would have been interesting – both for type theory and with applications to selection in mind – to investigate motives and expectations too.

TYPE DYNAMICS

Type dynamics is the level of type beyond the four preferences and the four letter types. The main idea is that in each type one of the central four prefer-ences (S, N, T or F) usually dominates the others. In normal type development this dominant function is used most and feels most comfortable; it is an essen-tial part of the person at their best. Type theory further assumes that extraverts use their dominant function mostly in the external world, because by definition that is where they are most comfortable, and introverts use theirs mostly in their inner world, for the same reason. Therefore we can think of the dominant func-tions as eight possible combinations: ES, IS, EN, IN, ET, IT, EF and IF. The idea of a dominant function is potentially of enormous value – if it is true and if it is applied well.

The next element in type dynamics may be equally valuable. It is that the opposite preference (or function) to the dominant is likely to be used least and that this too is likely to affect our behaviour – both what we do less well and less often and how we respond to stress. Several of the type descriptions, e.g. those of Myers (1993) and Hirsh and Kummerow (1990), include this element. Type and stress are discussed in Chapter 9.

The other elements in basic type dynamics are that the other preference of the middle two in a person's four letter type is the 'second-in-command' and that, for balance, it tends to be extraverted if the dominant function is introverted and vice versa; that its 'partner' is the third function; and that the opposite to the dominant is the fourth function (as implied above). Type theory therefore suggests a hierar-chy of functions in normal type development. The descriptions in the Report Form (Table 3.1) assume that the dominant function is the most developed, the auxiliary second and so on, that the dominant and auxiliary functions are both developed to a reasonable extent and that anxiety is average or below average.

The subtleties and complexities of type dynamics are discussed in detail by Quenk (1993) (see also Chapters 4 and 9 here). As they are also largely untested at present in any formal sense, I will first describe how to infer the dominant function from the four letter type, then discuss the evidence on the validity of this level of type theory and then move to the calmer, simpler approach of temperament theory.

The 'cookbook' way to deduce the dominant and other functions is to follow the formula:

Step one

If E and P, then S or N (whichever is in the four-letter type) is the dominant.
If E and J, then T or F is the dominant.
If I and J, then S or N.
If I and P, then T or F.

Step two

The fourth function is the opposite of the dominant.

Step three

The second function or auxiliary is whichever preference from S, N, T or F is in the four-letter type but is not the dominant.

Step four

The third function is the opposite of the second.

An example – ENFP

E and P so the dominant function is N and the fourth function is S. Second is F and third T. Moreover, because of E, the dominant function can more precisely be described as EN and the auxiliary as IF.

For a table giving all the dominants, etc. see Hirsh and Kummerow (1990, p. 9). They also suggest possible strengths of each dominant function and some of the possible consequences of each fourth function, which they call 'the inferior' (p. 10). For example, one suggested strength of dominant sensing is handling problems realistically; of thinking – analysing; of intuition – recognizing new possibilities; and of feeling – appreciating others (Hirsh and Kummerow, 1990, p. 10). Table 3.5 is a more detailed description of the strengths (in theory) of each dominant function.

Metaphors and similes may be a more appealing way of describing the dominant functions. An exercise that can work well with a fairly knowledgeable group is for dominant function groups to draw or paint images representing first their dominant and then their fourth function. Some groups want to devise images for other functions too. For example, an IF group produced an EF image that was much too bright and volcano-like for the EF group and illustrated a subtle aspect of type dynamics: that a dominant function (in this case, F) can be seen quite differently by people who use the same function in the opposite world.

Table 3.5: Dominant functions of each type and associated motives

Introverted sensing (ISJ)
To notice and work on something useful to others, quietly, systematically, and in depth.

Extraverted sensing (ESP)
To find excitement and fun.

Introverted intuition (INJ)
To imagine new ideas, systems and strategies and apply them.

Extraverted intuition (ENP)
To find *lots* of new and stimulating possibilities and promote new ventures.

Introverted thinking (ITP)
To analyse events or ideas in depth and create new designs, models and frameworks.

Extraverted thinking (ETJ)
To analyse, organize and control situations, solve problems (using established ideas and information) and get results.

Introverted feeling (IFP)
To find harmony and a sense of order, through working quietly and individually on something that matters (to the person).

Extraverted feeling (EFJ)
To help others to be happy.

It is rare for all the dominant functions to be represented in any one large group, but there will usually be examples of images for the same preference from one group as their dominant and from another group as their fourth function. Table 3.6 lists some verbal images from a variety of sources including Jean Kummerow, students on a counselling course and *The Type Reporter*.

Table 3.6: Metaphors and similes for the dominant functions

ES	Waves on a beach
IS	Filing cabinet; corridor with lots of rooms, each with a label
EN	Searchlight; swirling cloud, everything moving and interconnected; radar
IN	Kaleidoscope; stewpot, bubbling; white water rapids
ET	Tornado
IT	Maze; oyster
EF	Spring day after a shower
IF	Purr

The images in Table 3.6 are a mixture of process, structure and outcome. For example, 'purr' is an outcome image and 'tornado' and 'stewpot' seem to capture process, structure and outcome. Further steps are to find good images for all aspects of all the dominant functions and to spell out the strengths of the images, which may lead to better images, and so on.

The Cambridge Type Inventory (CTI; Rawling, 1994) is a new questionnaire which is intended to measure directly the direction of use of the dominant function (the MBTI attempts to measure direction of use indirectly). As Tables 3.5 and 3.6 illustrate, there is a large difference between, say, IS and ES. Rawling further suggests that the order and direction of the functions in many people are not as assumed in type theory, e.g. he finds that in some people dominant and auxiliary are both extraverted. However, this claim assumes the validity of the CTI, which is at present untested, and type theory would in any case interpret such a pattern as an example of one kind of false type development (discussed in Chapter 4 and touched on in the next section).

'Introverted complexity No. 47'

The title of this section is Kroeger's (undated) tongue-in-cheek title for an article on introverts. In the article, he develops an implication of the idea that introverts' dominant functions are introverted; he argues that there is inevitably a conflict between the demands of the external world and the time and space needed by the dominant, and that an overactive auxiliary and a neglected dominant may be the result. Moreover, everyone, including the introvert themselves, may believe that the auxiliary is actually the dominant, which would be another kind of false type development. Kroeger suggests two sets of diagnostic questions to try to prevent or at least recognize a neglected dominant. For IJs they are:

1. Do you find yourself pushed to finish what you start?
2. Do you have trouble setting yourself apart and relaxing?
3. Would you rather do a job yourself than trust it to someone else?
4. Would you rather schedule your private time rather than just let it happen?
5. Would you rather take charge of an event and move it towards completion?

For IPs, Kroeger suggests the following questions:

1. Do you find yourself following the moment?
2. Is your day more 'starts' than follow-throughs?
3. Is your life 'piles' of things to do someday?
4. Do you have trouble finding time for yourself?
5. Do your 'best laid plans often times go astray'?

He suggests that three or more 'yes' answers to the appropriate set of questions is a good indication that Introverted Complexity No. 47 is gaining on you – probably in an insidious way. It is easy to believe that the outside world is more important but introverts believe this at their peril and should not be 'led astray' – dominated – by their auxiliaries. Therefore IPs and those who know them benefit from their focusing on and finishing things most of the time (in a sense IPs are really Js) and IJs and those who know them benefit from their being unfocused and relaxed and not worrying about finishing things and schedules most of the time (in a sense IJs are really Ps).

No-one has published research on this aspect of type dynamics yet. It would require a good measure of stress, a group of IJs and IPs and perhaps an interview about dominant and auxiliary. Another implication is that it would sometimes be 'cleaner' to do research on dominant functions with extraverts only.

RESEARCH ON TYPE DYNAMICS

Most of the research on the MBTI has been on single preferences. However, the data on occupations and stress (both discussed in Chapter 9) are relevant to the validity of the types and so are Thorne and Gough (1991) and Harrison and Lawrence (1985).

Thorne and Gough (1991) had enough data (on 614 participants, over 30 years) to draw conclusions about ten of the types: the eight N types, ISTJs and ESTJs. Their book includes a table for each of the ten, listing the characteristics most and least associated with it, compared with all the other types (pp. 83–100). Thus for INFP females, the most characteristic description was 'Thinks and associates to ideas in unusual ways, has unconventional thought processes' (a relationship of 0.21 with observers' ratings), and the second most characteristic description was 'Is introspective and concerned with self as an object' (0.20). Thorne and Gough's general evaluation is that 'the trends for females correspond rather well to the discussion of INFPs in the MBTI Manual' (p. 82) but these two examples do not seem to me to support their view: rather, they seem consistent with N and I respectively more than with distinctive INFP qualities. Similarly, the adjectives most associated with INFP females were 'original' (0.16), 'artistic' (0.15) and 'lazy' (0.15), which are not obviously predicted by type theory to be the **most** characteristic qualities of INFPs (see the Report Form descriptions, Table 3.1).

Three general points about Thorne and Gough's research seem appropriate. First, they did find substantial and numerous differences between the types: 'In every instance, for all ten types for which our data were sufficient to permit analysis, characteristic combinations of strengths and weaknesses were discerned' (p. 101). Second, in some cases these differences relate to the types in a type dynamics sense and in others they do not. Third, the way the differences are described is often contaminated by value judgements and I suspect by situational effects, which makes interpretation difficult. For example, INFP males are described as tending to be 'snobbish' (0.18) and 'irritable' (0.17). I expect INFPs (male and female) to find it difficult to adjust to new situations, especially ones without a clear and attractive role, and it may be this character-istic that is reflected in judgements like 'snobbish'.

Overall, I think the Thorne and Gough data deserve a careful and systematic evaluation, distinguishing the 'loaded' descriptions from the more objective ones, taking type dynamics and the biases of USA culture, especially towards E and I, into account and then testing type theory where possible. Thorne and Gough have made a start at examining the implications of their findings for type theory, but only in one (usually the final) paragraph in each section. For exam-ple, taking a relatively straightforward example in terms of type dynamics, they comment:

> ENFJs are described by Myers and McCaulley (1985) as radiating warmth and fellowship, placing a high value on harmonious human contacts, appreciative of others' good qualities, and accepting of their opinions. Our empirical findings for both sexes are in agreement with this formula-tion'. (p. 94)

The predicted descriptions of ENFJs are then as predicted by type theory, with the most salient characteristic the expected one (see Tables 3.5 and 3.6). The predictions for the other E types are also largely supported. In contrast, predic-tions for the Is are largely not supported, which in itself is an interesting finding relevant to both cultural and temporal bias and to type dynamics. I will examine ISTJs in more detail, as an example.

Male and female ISTJs were both described as 'tends towards overcontrol of needs and impulses; delays gratification unnecessarily (0.16 and 0.25 respec-tively) (p. 91), and the suppressive, overcontrolled element – at least in the eyes of the particular observers – is evident in other ratings of most and least charac-teristic too. Thorne and Gough comment that there is a 'moderate correspon-dence' between MBTI descriptions and their findings but that the basis of the self-discipline 'seems to be more a fear of self-expression or impulse-release than a positive manifestation of pro-social dispositions' (p. 90), i.e. they contrast the ratings of the observers with type theory's (positive) view of ISTJs' motives.

I see their interpretation as an interesting hypothesis more than a finding. To the extent that it is a finding, it is based on only ten females (though 37 males) and in a particular setting and time, as emphasized earlier. Moreover, being primarily responsible, according to type theory, could result in fearfulness about expressing impulses, for example, rather than cause it and it may be possible to disentangle these two possibilities. At the same time, the observers did not detect a deep sense of responsibility as the major and basic characteristic of ISTJs, as predicted by type theory. More research is needed to explore both the characteristics of ISTJs and their underlying motives, whether fearful (Thorne and Gough) or positive (MBTI).

Harrison and Lawrence (1985) used type dynamics to predict the rank order of all 16 types on a task which asked them to write about their personal futures.

INTJs (dominant INs) were hypothesized to project themselves furthest into the future and ESFJs (dominant EF plus sensing) the least. The participants were 302 schoolchildren, matching the general population in proportions of the types. The INTJs and ENTPs projected themselves an average of 33 and 28 years respectively into the future, the ESFJs and ISFPs both 8 years, with all the other types very close to the order predicted.

These results are extraordinarily clear and demand to be replicated: a repeat of the correlation of 0.98 or anything like it, together with an absence of any flaws in the design (I can't see any), would provide further strong support for the meaningfulness of the notion of dominant functions. The authors point out that while their study supports the idea that N is related more than S, T or F to future orientation, it did not test the related ideas about F and a past orientation, S and the present, and T and a linear orientation, nor has any other research to date. It would also be of interest to investigate dominant function and past/future orientation in adults.

The same judgement applies to Garden's research on type and stress, discussed in Chapter 9.

KEIRSEY'S TEMPERAMENT THEORY

Temperament theory illustrates the interactive sense of the word 'type'. Like the idea of type dynamics, it goes beyond a simple additive model. Temperament theory assumes that the JP preference has a major effect on the behaviour of sensing types and a trivial effect on intuitive types and that the TF preference has a major effect on intuitive types and a minor effect on sensing types, hence the four temperaments: SP, SJ, NT and NF, with each including four MBTI types. No rationale is offered by Keirsey and Bates (1978) for these assumptions. Rather, they are presented as the result of observation and as supported by a long history of related attempts to devise useful typologies of character. Clearly, though, the starting point for temperament theory is SN.

Temperament theory can be seen as either a simpler way of interpreting the MBTI or as a separate theory, fortuitously overlapping type theory and being measured with the same questionnaire. I see it as supplementing the MBTI but also as challenging it. First, though, Table 3.7 outlines my interpretation of each temperament's basic motives. By 'basic' I mean 'most influential'. Almost everyone, for example, needs some security, but is one of the group of motives in Table 3.7 the **most** important, the one you would not give up – at least not for long – given the choice? Bear in mind that the importance of each motive in each temperament is a matter of degree, just as most people need time alone but generally introverts need more than extraverts. For detailed descriptions of the temperaments, see Keirsey and Bates (1978) and Brownsword (1987). Figures 3.1, 3.2, 3.3 and 3.4 provide a concise summary. See also Tables 7.3, 9.3, 9.4, 9.6 and 9.7.

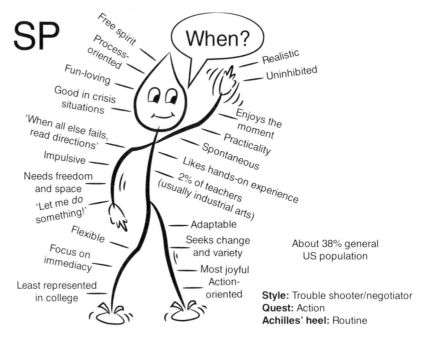

Figure 3.1 Typical SP characteristics (© Otto Kroeger Associates).

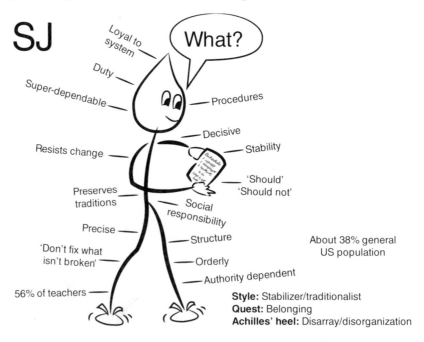

Figure 3.2 Typical SJ characteristics (© Otto Kroeger Associates).

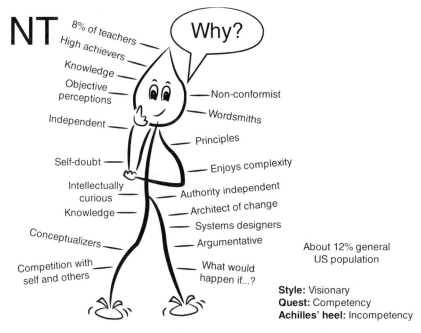

Figure 3.3 Typical NT characteristics (© Otto Kroeger Associates).

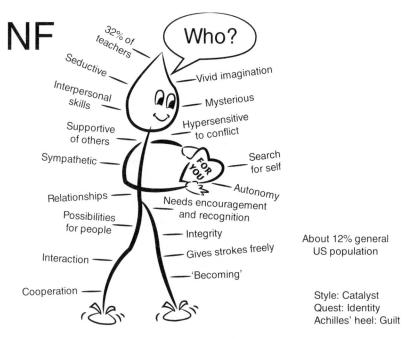

Figure 3.4 Typical NF characteristics (© Otto Kroeger Associates).

Table 3.7: Basic motives for each temperament (developed from Keirsey and Bates, 1978)

SP	—	Excitement and adventure
	—	Responding to crises
	—	Flexibility and freedom
SJ	—	Being responsible and useful
	—	Planning in detail
	—	Stability and security
NT	—	Developing new theories/models/ideas/systems
	—	Analysis, criticism and understanding
	—	Competence
NF	—	Harmony
	—	Self-development
	—	Supporting other people

Table 3.8 shows percentages of the temperaments, based on MBTI types, in four groups. Keirsey's own estimates are stated with characteristic authority (and unlikely symmetry) and without any information on where he got them from, but are fairly similar to the USA general population figures, and to the UK data. They are 38% SPs, 38% SJs, 12% NTs, 12% NFs. The data from the two psychology classes at the University of East London (Table 3.8) provide a comparison.

Table 3.8: Approximate percentages of the temperaments in four groups

	SP	SJ	NT	NF
General population (USA) 1985 N = 9500*	22	44	16	18
Large public sector organization (UK) 1992 N = 496 (males)**	33	52	8	6
Psychology class UEL Yr 1 1990 N = 104	11	12	30	47
Psychology class UEL Yr 1 1993 N = 120	13	24	29	34

*Calculated from Table 3.3
**Calculated from Table 3.4

Type and temperament theory appear to clash in some respects. For example, temperament is a theory of behaviour and so while ISTJs have introverted S as their (not very visible) dominant, they are also SJs, and visibly so. Moreover, SJs tend to be very focused on goals yet dominant IS is playful and flexible. A further difference is that temperament theory does not have a model of development, other than people becoming increasingly like their temperament as they get older.

The challenge to type theory from temperament theory can be further illustrated with the ISFP/INFP types. In Myers' theory both are introverted feeling types with much in common; in Keirsey's theory, they are SPs and NFs respectively, with little in common. There is clearly scope for research here, both conceptual and empirical. My view is that both theories are useful and that it is probably best to live with the contradictions (which may be resolvable) until we have more good evidence. So far there is little formal research on temperament theory (for a review, see Frisbie, 1988). Keirsey and Bates (1978) is rich with anecdotes and clinical impressions but with no interest shown in more rigorous forms of evidence.

Temperament theory is supported indirectly and in general terms by much of the research on the MBTI, though no-one has yet reviewed the research from this viewpoint. For applications of temperament theory in education and organizations, see Chapters 8 and 9 respectively.

OTHER INTERACTIONS BETWEEN THE PREFERENCES

Frisbie (1988), as part of a critique of temperament theory, proposed that a more fruitful fourfold approach would be combinations of the functions: ST, SF, NT, NF (see Tables 8.3 and 8.4). Myers and McCaulley (1985, pp. 31–8) offered hypotheses about several other combinations, e.g. IP, EP, IJ, EJ. It seems likely that some of these combinations will prove to be important for some purposes, but I think testing other aspects of type theory is a clear priority.

CONCLUSIONS

1. Type dynamics, in which the preferences are seen as interacting with each other, is a more speculative but potentially very valuable aspect of type theory, as illustrated by 'Introverted Complexity No. 47', for example.
2. The key idea of the dominant function is supported by the perceived validity of the type descriptions and up to a point (and particularly for extraverts) by Thorne and Gough's (1991) data. Testing the value of the idea of a dominant function is a priority for further research.
3. I agree with Keirsey (e.g. Keirsey and Bates, 1978), Brownsword (1987) and others that type and temperament complement each other rather than being rivals, much as type and the EAR do, but at some point this general harmony will need examining closely.

<table>
<tr><td>**4**</td><td># Type development</td></tr>
</table>

Psychological type theory includes a model of lifelong personality development which – with type dynamics – provides a strong counterargument to the criticism that it 'puts people in boxes'. The model needs examining in depth by a developmental psychologist with a special interest in personality. In earlier chapters, I touched on some of the relevant areas: the interaction between inherited predisposition and early environment in Chapter 1, the effects of cultural expectations on thinking women and feeling men in Chapter 2. This chapter is in two main sections. In the first, I briefly discuss the following aspects of type development:

1. good type development;
2. false type development;
3. can type development be 'speeded up'? And if so, how?
4. can type development be measured?

The second section is an updated (February 1994) version of a 1985 article by Jean Kummerow on her own type development as an ESTJ. I asked Jean if I could include her article because it is the clearest, most absorbing account of type development that I have come across. It brings the theory alive on three levels: general, ESTJs and one ESTJ in particular.

GOOD TYPE DEVELOPMENT

Type theory assumes that very few people are able to use all eight preferences easily and appropriately, even after using them for most of their lives. It also assumes that equal development of all the functions is not desirable: that the dominant function should be the most developed function, the auxiliary the second most developed in each type, and so on. Myers suggested the analogy of trying to listen to two radio stations on the same wavelength (1980, pp. 182–3) for trying to develop both S and N or T and F at the same time. Jung took the same view: 'It is practically impossible ... for anyone to develop all [their] psychological functions simultaneously' (1923, para 763).

However, the radio analogy does not stand up for long – different stations can be heard with equal clarity at different times and informal observation suggests that some people develop one or more of their non-preferred functions in the same period of their life as their dominant and auxiliary, and sometimes when they are young. There are considerable individual differences in how many preferences are developed, to what extent and when.

On the other hand, it is feasible that it is not possible to be interested in, for example, both what is happening (S) and in possibilities (N) at the same time and that this tends to lead to one mode being used more, trusted more and more developed, and so on, in a cumulative and spiral pattern and the other being shut off and neglected. Indeed it needs to be the case for type to be valid.

The assumption here is that a firm sense of self or identity actually requires this kind of consistency and therefore a choice between each of the pairs of preferences. Each chosen and developed preference then acts as a kind of 'anchor' for a person's identity. Olson (1993), writing as an ESFJ about her role as president of the predominantly NP Association of Psychological Type, put this well:

> I have confidence to take risks to be true to my own style when I'm in a 'foreign land' of intuitives. I know I can't be an intuitive president; that would be a falsification of who I am. Instead, I can be a sensing president who uses intuition. (p. 3)

Good development further assumes that balance in another sense, between different kinds of function, is desirable. In Myers' words:

> The need for such supplementing is obvious. Perception without judgment is spineless; judgment with no perception is blind. Introversion lacking any extraversion is impractical; extraversion with no introversion is superficial. (1980, p. 182)

Perhaps the only word out of place in Myers' characteristic summary is 'impractical'; 'dormant' might have been closer to her meaning. This assumption of the need for a balance between the perceiving and judging functions and between E and I seems feasible too: everyone takes in information and comes to conclusions about it and everyone behaves introvertedly sometimes and extravertedly at other times.

The general picture in normal type development is of each person gradually discovering what they are best at – their talents, gifts and central motives – and what is 'not them'. We then spend more time and energy on what we are best at and necessarily less on other things. But type theory also suggests that development of the dominant and auxiliary, at least in some people, reaches a kind of ceiling and then more attention is paid to the third and fourth functions (in this order). For example, some ENFPs, who have been primarily imaginative and enthusiastic, do not become ISTJs but do reach a time when they find reflection, logic, analysis and/or planning more attractive (Myers, 1980, Corlett and

Millner, 1993). Provost (1984, p.4) suggests that 'If and when No. 4 (and No. 3) can be utilized in mature adulthood, the outcome is often positive, even exhilarating'. I suspect that this is true more often for some types (ENPs?) than others and that some 'mature adults' do not develop their third or fourth preferences to the extent Provost suggests, despite opportunity, but become more and more like their types. Similarly, Olson (1993) suggested in passing that perhaps only Ns have midlife crises.

Theories of personality which include a concept of real self or basic tendencies usually include ideas about how these can be realized and about obstacles (see the section on pp. 7–11 on 'preference'). For example for a child to have close relationships with a variety of people – all the temperaments, for example – might be a positive factor (Storr, 1960) and later in life too. A phrase of John Updike's put this well: 'We contain chords which others must strike'. Rogers emphasizes the quality of relationships more than their variety, especially how empathic, accepting and genuine they are (e.g. Rogers, 1961).

The best sources of specific applications of type theory to child development are in the later chapters of Murphy (1992) and two series of articles by Scanlon (1991 and 1992–3). Murphy's applications of type to teaching are reviewed in Chapter 8.

Scanlon (1991) argued that mothers try to be too ideal and tend to concentrate on their failings. A type theory approach is to help each mother focus on her strengths more than her failings and to look after herself as well as others. (Fathers are peripheral in this series of articles but the ideas apply equally to them.)

Scanlon lists five positive outcomes for herself and her family from seminars by Janet Penley and Diane Stephens called M.O.M.S. (Mothers of Many Styles):

1. greater confidence as a mother. The positive description of Scanlon as an INFJ mother has stayed with her;
2. less critical of other mothers. There are different kinds of good mother;
3. less critical of her own mother. Children benefit from the type framework too;
4. her husband became less critical of himself as a father;
5. taking care of her own needs more, e.g. telling her children 'I just need about a half hour to be alone, and then I'll feel more like playing with you'.

Scanlon discusses each type's strengths as a mother. Many of them, of course, are those listed as the strengths of the dominant functions in Table 3.5 and of the preferences in counselling in Table 7.3.

Scanlon (1992–3) interviewed parents about the problems they'd like help with and contrasts the views of 'The Old Codger', who treats all children the same, with a type perspective from Elizabeth Murphy. For example, one parent said her eight year old intuitive son keeps coming up with fantastic, impossible ideas and keeps being disappointed. The Old Codger says 'Children have to learn not to ask for crazy things. Just keep telling him to stop being so unrealistic or he'll never get what he wants!' Murphy's view is that the son needs help to translate his dreams into projects. 'Don't get hung up on the impossibility of the idea. Use it to begin a process of exploration.' For example, the child could draw a picture of it or divide a page into two with 'Possibles' on one side and 'Probables' on the other. 'Explain that the possible column is for all his good ideas and the probable column is for what you (i.e. the son) think the two of you can actually do.' Sometimes a possibility now will be a probable in a few years' time (Scanlon 1992–3).

There is very little research on type development (though I suspect there is much that is relevant in the literature on developmental psychology) and hardly any theory about the third function (Quenk, 1993). The fourth function though, as indicated earlier, is much speculated about: it can be seen as a part of ourselves we tend to 'confront' in midlife, as something we mostly avoid but can be 'hooked' by, that can attack us, fascinate us and sometimes 'spins us around' (Jung, 1923, para 85).

The section on conscious development of the preferences on pp. 64–7 lists some activities intended to 'stretch' each preference (Tables 4.1 and 4.2). Type theory suggests, though, a crucial difference between developing true type and developing one's 'other side': developing the dominant and auxiliary is like 'coming home', while with the other preferences there is always a sense of effort.

FALSE TYPE DEVELOPMENT

If a true preference is actively discouraged for long enough (type theory seems to see the preferences as sufficiently robust to resist lack of encouragement), then a false type develops. For Jung and Myers, the consequences for the individual are less effective behaviour, a sense of 'not being right' and possibly acute exhaustion and neurosis (Jung, 1923, paras. 560–1).

It is easy to picture environmental factors that can impede or suppress type development: a T child who is not allowed to argue, an I who is not allowed time alone, an S who is expected to learn only through words. These examples confound two processes: discouraging the child from using their natural preferences and encouraging them (probably with love and good intentions) to use the other preferences. Myers refers to 'falsification of type', a process 'which robs its victims of their real selves and makes them into inferior, frustrated copies of other people' (1980, p. 189). Various patterns of false type development are logically possible, e.g. initially developing the functions in a different order from the one proposed by the theory but later in life recovering to the 'right' order.

CAN TYPE DEVELOPMENT BE SPEEDED UP?

Two obvious questions about type development are: 'Can it be speeded up?'

and 'If so, how?' One answer to the first question is 'Yes, when there has been false type development'. But that leaves the problem of whether, in normal development, it is desirable to 'forcefeed' a natural process. If there is normal type development, it may be best to let it continue to happen at its own pace. One possible disadvantage of conscious attempts to speed up development is feeling pressured to be perfect or, of course, developing 'too fast' and missing out on what may be the intrinsic pleasures of developing at a 'natural' pace.

However, I will assume that some conscious intent and action to develop one's type is a reasonable and attractive option and Tables 4.1 and 4.2 list some strategies. A further consideration is that logic (yet to be tested by research) suggests that significant development of all the **attitudes** is more basic than development of all the **functions**. It hardly seems possible to live without developing some E (though Es may perhaps manage better without I) and being only J or only P would similarly be too extreme a handicap. Nothing would be done or too many things would be done too quickly. In contrast, some people seem to cope fairly well without obvious development of one or two of the functions (S, N, T and F), though there are of course consequences for themselves and others and at some point (theoretically, midlife) pressures from within and from life events might demand some attention for the neglected functions (Quenk, 1993; Corlett and Milner, 1993).

Table 4.1: Examples of strategies for developing EI and JP (the attitudes)

E	Speak spontaneously
	Discuss something without preparing (cf. Rogers' concept of 'unrehearsed speech')
	Talk to an audience
	Introduce yourself to someone you don't know
I	Spend undistracted time alone
	Stay quiet in a group
	Work alone on a project
J	Make a list of things to do, put them in order of priority, and do the first one
	Make a plan
P	Spend unplanned time, following impulses
	Re-examine a final decision

An exercise for working systematically on type development is outlined next. To use this exercise, the interviewer, the trainer or yourself needs to be familiar with listening and challenging skills (e.g. Bayne *et al.*, 1994) and with type

Table 4.2: Examples of strategies for developing SN and TF (the functions)

S	Observe something carefully, e.g. non-verbal behaviour (E), nature (E), your inner physical state (I)
	Eat slowly and with concentration (I)
	Massage (EI), dance (E), housework (E)
	Do anything that requires attention to detail (E)
	List all the facts about something (E)
	Describe an activity, step by step (E)
N	Brainstorm (I)
	Daydream or fantasize (I)
	Imagine five years ahead (I)
	Design something new (E)
T	Devise a flowchart (I)
	List the costs and benefits of a decision (I)
	Tell someone what you find difficult about them (E)
	Define something precisely (I)
F	Clarify your values (I)
	Empathize (E)
	Use more emotion words (I)
	Compliment someone on their appearance or personality (E)
	List things you like and dislike (I)

theory. The information needed is as follows.

1. An MBTI result, preferably a verified result, as described in Chapter 2.
2. A list of characteristics for each preference (Tables 2.4, 2.6, 2.8 and 2.10).
3. A flowchart (Figure 4.1).
4. The following instructions.

Instructions for the type development exercise

The exercise asks you to explore two questions: 'Do I experience/behave in this way?' and 'Do I want to experience/behave **more** in this way?'

1. Work in pairs or threes, taking turns to be the 'client' and 'interviewer(s)', or on your own.
2. Take the list of characteristics describing your dominant function and use the flowchart. Bear in mind that if you are extraverted, the characteristics of the dominant function will in theory apply more to your behaviour, while if you are introverted they will apply more to your inner experience.

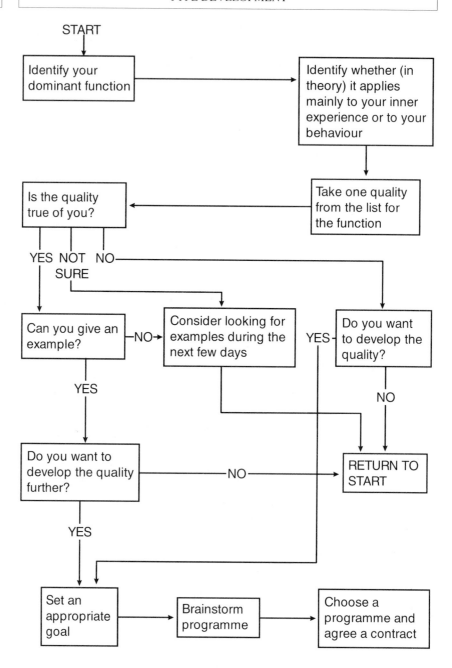

Figure 4.1 Flowchart for self-development exercise (from Bayne, 1988b).

3. The contract (bottom right of the flowchart) is about when and how the action stage is carried out. For example, a client might decide she wanted to develop her introverted feeling further and to do this by carrying out a values clarification exercise on Tuesday.
4. One or two programmes of action at a time per client is enough.
5. Several variations of the exercise can be used, e.g. to work on developing the auxiliary, third or fourth functions or directly on one or more of the attitudes, whichever the client wishes. Some clients have no desire at all to work on their dominant function but want more 'balance' through developing their auxiliary.
6. Feedback and discussion, taking the types of both or all of you into account.

The flowchart is an example of type development itself, since the person who drew it was a dominant F and flowcharts seem a T skill. It is, however, significant that although I enjoyed doing it (I am an INFP), it was several years ago and it is still my only flowchart.

Two other variations of the exercise are to leave out the action stage and treat it as a self-awareness/self-esteem activity, rather than self-development, and to choose pairs according to type, e.g. both with the same dominant function.

MY POLY-ACTIVE DESK

'Poly-active' is one of the EAR elements of P: it means doing several things at once, jumping from task to task and having many other things to do, some untouched for months or more, etc. The contrasting J quality is called Stress Avoider and includes a preference for doing one thing at a time and not forgetting it until it is done. Poly-active people **like** to do several things at once: it's exciting and leads to unexpected links. They also respond well to and feel more creative under pressure from deadlines. Stress Avoiders try to reduce this kind of stress by starting early.

As another example of type development (this time of J by a P) I learned to control the poly-active part of my preference for P a little better through the following lucky incident. When I worked in the Civil Service, my desk top was always a sea of papers but one day a request came around to keep our desk tops clear so that they could be renewed. It took weeks for the renewal to actually happen and in that time I discovered, after a lifetime of clutter, that having a clear desk helped me focus more and that I liked it. I extended the skill to books; rather than read ten at once, I try to finish with one before starting another. I haven't lost my poly-active 'true self' but I have learned – fortuitously – to work more effectively through adding some of the opposing J skills.

CAN TYPE DEVELOPMENT BE MEASURED?

To carry out research on type development, we need to be able to measure it. The MBTI is definitely not intended to do this. Indeed, the distinction between preferences on the one hand and abilities, skills and how well developed the preferences are on the other, is a crucial feature in interpreting MBTI results. Comparing scores **between** each person is a misuse. At one time, I thought the numerical element of MBTI results could be used to indicate the relative development of the preferences **within** each person, but no longer believe this happens enough of the time to be useful. Interpretation of the number part of MBTI results is discussed in Chapter 5.

What is needed are performance measures – both typical and maximum – for each preference. How good is this person at behaving extravertedly? How long does she typically sustain it? How comfortable is she behaving in this way? How extravert can she comfortably be on a particular occasion? It is easier to think of measures for some of the preferences than others. High level cognitive tests would measure some aspects of developed thinking, for example. In contrast, so-called 'creativity' tests (for N) and 'empathy' tests (for F) are still controversial.

The Personality Assessment System (PAS) (Krauskopf and Saunders, 1994) is another possibility. This method interprets profiles of ability test scores, e.g. an arithmetic subtest which is related to thinking. The system is, however, very complicated. It attempts to measure three levels of personality and distinguishes between 64 basic personality types and 512 personality configurations. Rather than introduce lots of new terms, I want simply to note the PAS and its apparent compatibility with type, e.g. as a categorizing measure and in its language. For type development, its significance is that the three levels of personality are the Primitive (innate tendencies), Basic (personality in adolescence) and Surface (later modifications) and that each characteristic at each level is measured with an ability test. Like the MBTI, the PAS assumes that the Basic type cannot be changed, only added to or suppressed.

Scanlon (1990a) translated some of the PAS subtests into MBTI terms. For example, EI in childhood appears to be measured best by the Picture Arrangement test, which asks people to put cards with pictures of interacting people on them in sequence. Es are seen as more aware of social roles and with a wider repertoire. SN in childhood is measured with the Digit Span test, repeating a list of unrelated numbers. Ns are able on average to store more numbers and repeat them. TF is measured by Block Design – the person looks at several designs and then attempts to duplicate them in coloured blocks. Ts do this in an analytic way and more quickly, Fs more impressionistically and relatively slowly. JP is measured with two tests. In the first, the person is asked to guess when 20 seconds are up, without counting in their head. Js tend to under- and Ps to overestimate. The second test presents a series of words describing colours, e.g. red, but the words themselves are in different colours, e.g. the word 'red' might be in blue. The task is to say the colour the word is written in, and Ps tend to do this more easily.

Quite apart from the validity of the PAS as a measure of type development, there is lots of scope for interesting and useful research in such ideas and findings – to measure the preferences and clarify their nature and to test the ideas of type dynamics. The PAS, like the MBTI, has been used primarily in clinical and applied work.

Scanlon sees the PAS as picking up 'where the theory of psychological type leaves off. The PAS seems to measure the same characteristics that the MBTI does although it describes them in slightly different ways ... it's really a measure of "type development"' (1990a, p. 1). She presents a case study of someone (Bob) who could not find a best fit MBTI type. The first finding was that Bob's IQ was extremely high, which suggests the capacity for greater 'role versatility' whatever the person's type. The argument here is that if someone is unusually capable in a general sense, weaknesses will not be the useful source of self-knowledge which they are for nearly everyone. Second, the PAS suggested significant differences between Bob's Primitive and Basic types.

CONCLUSIONS

1. Type theory makes several assumptions about the order in which the preferences normally develop, the desirability of there being one function which is dominant, the consequences of false type development and so on. These assumptions, and ideas about the 'ideal' parent, on which type theory provides a useful perspective, need further analysis and testing.
2. Some methods for conscious development of each preference were outlined. The question of whether conscious attempts to increase the rate of type development have negative effects in some or all circumstances is an open one.
3. The PAS seems promising as a measure of type development and as a source of ideas and measures for research on other aspects of type theory.

TYPE DEVELOPMENT FROM AN ESTJ PERSPECTIVE (JEAN KUMMEROW)

Background note

This section is based on a panel presentation on type development at the International Association for Psychological Type Conference in June 1985 in Evanston, Illinois, USA. I was in my mid-30s thinking I had a handle on what had been and what was to come in terms of my type development. When Rowan Bayne asked if he could include my article in his book I requested the opportunity to update it; much has happened to my understanding of type development and of me since then. I am now in my mid-40s (with more knowledge, I hope) and realize that one can never have a complete handle on type development, just an understanding at some point of what has happened/is happening.

To put this in context, the first version of this was an oral presentation and I've kept that style here. The original panel consisted of six people, mostly of Intuitive types, and the audience was overwhelmingly Intuitive; I was the only representative of the ST column and the ES quadrant but joined by a representative of the SJ temperament. Thus, I felt a great responsibility to represent not only my type well, but also my column and quadrant.

> When Naomi [Quenk] first called and invited me to be on this panel, I was first aware of the strong sense of *responsibility* I felt in attempting to help you all understand my type and our type development. Then when I discovered the make-up of this panel, my sense of responsibility escalated – not only was I responsible for explaining ESTJs, but also for representing the ST column and the ES quadrant.
>
> As you might guess, I consider responsibility to be a key point in understanding ESTJs. What I say I will do, I will do and I will try to do it as efficiently as possible, of course. It is almost as if I have made a sacred oath when I agree to do something – when I say it out loud to others, I mean it. As a child, I felt so responsible to do everything right. I would spend untold hours making sure my school assignments were perfect and on time. I could not understand people who would not follow through. In my own critical way, I would assume they were either liars who deliberately broke their promises or they were dumb because they forgot their promises. You will be glad to hear I have learned much more understanding and forgiveness since then.
>
> I suppose the question with ESTJs really becomes what are they responsible for? The first responsibility, quite frankly, is to get the job done properly. We would rather not talk about it, we would rather do it. Of course, part of our type development is learning to value the process or way a job is to be done and that means, too, the people involved, along with the actual completion of the job. One of my favorite tasks in life is to help NPs move into action by helping them get organized and off dead center through encouraging them to move ideas to implementation.
>
> You may have heard me say the word 'organized'. Yes, ESTJs are organized and we are planful. How I do it, I do not know ... I just am organized. In grade school, I would always do my homework first and then work on my Girl Scout badges. (I earned a lot of badges!) Now my husband, John, who is an INFP, says I am not really that well organized. When I ask him about his particular concerns, it turns out they are my very low priorities. I do not care to organize how the house looks, what meals we're going to eat and how I dress. I do care about having a smooth flowing business and getting the children to school and to their outside activities on time. In other words, I have just organized myself into clear priorities and what he sees as poorly organized are at the bottom of my list.

For many people, part of being organized is following a standard oper-
ating procedure. That certainly is true for me, unless those procedures are
inefficient, illogical, stupid and/or they simply do not work. I will follow
decent procedures, in fact I kind of like them. I do not like to reinvent the
wheel and find redoing and reinventing things that already exist to be an
awful waste of time. Lists are great ways of keeping me on track and
keeping track of what I need to do. There are very few days ever when I
do not have a list, even when I'm on holiday.

ESTJs' dominant function is extraverted thinking. Some people say we
appear somewhat cold, calculating and detached. I prefer to look at it as
objective, logical and focused; I enjoy making decisions. I like people to
give me reasons for things and I have a hard time accepting an answer
unless it is logical. I like being in situations where I can analyze and
critique and make decisions. In fact, for me not to be able to critique is
exceedingly difficult; I love to be picky, about the right things of course,
but there are times when I am concerned that I sound too critical and
negative in the process.

One thing I enjoy doing is writing and critiquing my own and others'
writing. This led to the nickname of the 'Slasher' in one organization for
which I worked; whenever they needed a piece of writing tightened up,
they would bring it to me and I would do the job! That nickname eventually led me to an editing job with Consulting Psychologists Press; I took
over a career anthology book project that had become stalled. Yes, we got
it done with some slashing and on time!

For me, my thinking is supreme. It's as if I have a 'decision tree' in my
head – I can branch to the logical task side or I can branch to the relationships side. I always branch to that logical side; I can't help it. It's like
those divining sticks held by someone searching for water in the desert.
There's an irresistible pull when water is underneath the sand and there's
an irresistible pull toward that logic.

I have learned that I must at some point pay attention to that people side
but to remember to do it is hard. I've named the necessary action as my
'circle the wagons' time. (I used to have a fixation on pioneer women
settling the West; they were in those wagon trains meeting each challenge
head on and in practical ways. They would move their wagons into a
circle to protect themselves from outside forces. It was through joining
forces and forging relationships that they were able to get the task of
protection done.) I always make sure that by the end of the project, I've
talked with each person personally to thank them for their contributions to
the task and in this way I've made sure my circle has included everyone
and thus we're all protected.

My extraverted thinking feels so easy, wonderful and multifaceted to
me. I can put logical structure on things ... I can critique ... I can find
flaws in advance ... I can see the pluses and minuses to anything ... I can

see to the core of the matter ... I can eliminate the fluff ... I can be quickly decisive ... I can analyze thoroughly ...

My auxiliary function is my introverted sensing. One of the ways I enjoy using that function is through reading and research. I simply lose myself to the quiet of that introverted side and feel a real sense of peacefulness of purpose. I love to gather facts whether that be the research portion of a paper or the details of the political climate in a company or the results of career inventories. I like to sit down, ponder the data, pull it together, reorder it for even greater logic and look for connections. But I do not gather facts for the heck of it – there has to be a practical and logical need for the data.

I like details and I find a certain satisfaction from having those details and facts organized. I like to be prepared. I seldom make errors of fact and I have a good memory. I like to remember people and their types. However, now that I'm in my mid-40s, I've noted that my brain cells for some of that detail seem full to capacity. I can no longer remember this information readily.

When I know what I am doing, I am good at giving directions and I like to give directions. My S and T work hand in hand in my directions. My INFP husband, John, and I were driving to his mother's house one day which is about two miles from ours. John has a tendency to daydream and forget to turn soon enough to make the trip as efficiently as possible. We might even go an extra few blocks! When I pointed out the turn to him, I think my exact words were 'Aren't you going to turn here!'; he said, 'You know Jean, if you continue to give me directions all the rest of our lives, you are never going to know if or when I get Alzheimer's disease.'

I also like to do sensing things such as balancing our checkbook. John will never understand the satisfaction I get through looking at all the details of our financial life and coming up with a bottom line sum even when that sum is negative. He is particularly disturbed that I do this on Friday nights when I should just be starting to enjoy the weekend. For me, it is when the things I am responsible for are organized that I can start to enjoy life.

Some of my sensing delights come through traveling and noticing and experiencing new things. I love the details of a place. My first trip to England was in 1963; I still recall vividly the red tile roofs and the green grass I could see from the air flying into Heathrow. Now that I fly into Gatwick for my trips to England, I miss those red tile roofs, but at least I have my memory of them. To make my trips to Oxford even more memorable, I set a goal to visit every one of the 35 colleges; I even set logical parameters to a visit – I had to see at least two quadrangles or the equivalent in each college. (Notice how I put sensing into a logical framework.) Yes, that goal has been met. Now on to Cambridge ...! In North America, I've set a goal of working in every state of the USA and every province of

Canada. (For those interested, I'm over half way there!) And I'm open to suggestions for experiential goals. My sensing too seems like a good friend to me.

My tertiary function is my intuition and I find I both extravert and introvert it depending on the circumstances. My understanding of my tertiary has grown much in the last decade; it is starting to have more facets to it but not as many as intuitives would have. I am not brilliant with intuitions, connections and seeing that big picture. I eventually find the big picture with my S and T much more often than I quickly see it. When I was younger, the essay portions of exams that asked me to conceptualize were always difficult. However, I studied long and hard and got enough facts together including other people's theories so I could at least throw in enough data and hope that they fit together enough to show a bit of intuition. I no longer take essay exams (thank goodness!), but I do write essays and find I must make extra efforts to make sure the themes I want are there and the big picture is apparent.

I confess reading most theories leaves me cold. I do not think ever in my lifetime I will be able to grasp left brain, right brain concepts. Please, that is not meant to challenge anyone to try. I do not want to learn the stuff. I have found myself compelled (and even interested) to look more at theories recently because I believe theories are a good way to summarize my own and others' experiences; in this way they have a logical purpose.

Luckily for me there are lots of ideas people running around the world, and many of them write and talk about their ideas. I simply collect them and adapt them. I love coming up with little twists on things other people have already thought of. I use my intuition to adapt things, to make them better. I also use it to be zany at times, to come up with playful turns of events.

As a sensing psychologist, I used to feel terribly inferior amongst my intuitive colleagues because I didn't see what they saw. I didn't trust my sense of what was going on to make connections with the themes in people's lives. But now I do. I suddenly gain insights on what is happening with people. Analogies appear in my head and I see pictures which my clients find valuable. My ISFP client is describing two possible career choices: in my pictures, one lacks a core but has many trappings on the periphery and one has a core that radiates warmth; I describe these pictures and my client knows instantly which career is for him. (Warmth!) What an experience! Intuition is starting to have some facets for me; it feels less like a chore.

My inferior function is my introverted feeling function and that is a hard one for me. Many people describe ESTJs as lacking in emotions and feelings. How wrong they are! We care, we have emotions and feelings, but remember we also introvert them. They are different than the other aspects of our lives which we do control more firmly.

[**Note:** I do not mean to equate feelings with emotions, but I believe feeling types pay more attention to their emotions and trust them more than thinking types. Their emotions are guides to their values and hence their decisions. Thinking types keep their emotions at arm's length and don't let them guide their decisions quite as much. We need to learn what they mean, but for us they have been more unreliable.]

Luckily, I am clear on my basic values; I was raised by an INFP mother who instilled strong human welfare values early on and to whom I am forever grateful. My upbringing was very affirming of me. My entire family have IN preferences: my mother, INFP; my father, INTJ; my older brother, INTP; and my younger sister, INTJ. I think my parents somehow sensed I was different from them and always encouraged my extraverted development, perhaps because they thought it was something they had struggled with in growing up. They passed on to me a great deal of N and F. My father, as an immigrant to the United States, got a chance because of American values. If he had remained in Europe, he would have been an unskilled laborer; in the United States, he became a university professor. Yes, N and F, giving people chances, recognizing uniqueness and making a difference in people's lives was/is important. But I act upon those in an ST manner.

I chose a career as a psychologist partly out of my human welfare value system. When I applied for graduate school, I applied for a counseling and student personnel program. I had planned to be a college administrator, not a counselor or therapist. My graduate program, however, was not what it appeared to be and actually was counseling training. I can still feel the lumps in my stomach listening to people explain their problems to me. At that time, I could not trust my own F enough to feel good about helping others. It was scary. Yet that experience was also incredibly broadening, but one I did not fully understand until I learned the Myers–Briggs several years later. Jobs in university administration did not exist when I completed my degree and I moved my career to management consulting, career counseling and training which seems a better use of my ST.

In spite of my clear sense of values, I still have a great deal of trouble with the F side in consistently appreciating my own and others' value (which is different than appreciating values) and also in recognizing when my F is out of control. I can be quite impatient. Being a parent has been a help here, especially with two children different than me. My daughter prefers ISFJ and my son, ISTP. Years ago my daughter taught me how she feels around my extraverted nature. She wanted to know if 'extraverts are people who ask questions that are none of their business'. My children continually remind me of what's important in life.

I am in midlife and my F is getting more attention, some deliberate, some not. My F has always snuck up on me in a variety of situations. I may get goose bumps describing a particularly meaningful interaction with a client. I feel tears of pride when one of my children does something special. I used to attempt to either ignore those signs or logically analyze them. Now I try to let those emotions and feelings be clues to my F, just be for a short period of time and acknowledge their existence. Next I start to logically analyze them to bring meaning; then they make sense. But their origins are very different than what I'm used to.

There have been several 'events' in the past years which seem to be leading me toward development. When my grandmother suffered a stroke several years ago and was unable to communicate, I instinctively took her hand and started telling her all my happy memories of her; she started to cry and I did too. I got to tell her goodbye in a very meaningful way. A good friend's cancer has returned and she is reminding me of life and what's important just by her example.

My children have reached adolescence where they no longer want a focus on them in the ways they had needed before; my husband is in a new emotional place with his life and his own exploration. Thus, my focus is shifting, but to what? Perhaps to me and my inner life instead of on them and my outer life. I have begun to reach out to old friends who had been put aside for my own family and work responsibilities as a way of nurturing my inner life. I am especially enjoying my female friends when earlier I enjoyed the company of my male friends more.

I recently participated in an imagery session. I have never felt comfortable with visualization techniques and was bothered by this for only one reason. What if I should get cancer and need to use visualizations and imagery for the cure ... what would I do? (Such is the mind of a practical ESTJ!) In this session and subsequent ones I was able to visualize all four of my functions and found all had much meaning for me. My visualization of my fourth function was that of a glacier melting. Yes, slowly my feeling was being exposed no matter what I did!

The feeling function is still amorphous for me; I don't even know its facets but I'm understanding and accepting F more. It's much easier to describe it intellectually than to face it intrapsychically.

One question I was asked after my presentation is 'How did it feel to reveal so much of myself?'. Off the top of my head I said, 'Fine, after all, I have been through counselor training where that was expected and therefore done'. But upon reflection, I realized that getting to F still brought up different uncomfortable feelings, lumps in my throat or whatever, when I chose to pay attention. I did not/could not reveal all of those inner feelings to an audience nor even to myself. There's much still to be done with my F and for me it's internal private work.

In closing, I'd like to point out a key characteristic ESTJs have. We set a goal and go after it. My goal was to briefly explain ESTJs through one ESTJ's path of development. I hope I have.

5

Criticisms and queries

In this chapter I discuss ten criticisms of type theory and the MBTI and nine queries about them. The criticisms are:

1. type and MBTI results are an insult to individuality;
2. behaviour is different in different situations;
3. the descriptions are too vague and general;
4. the MBTI Report Form descriptions are too positive;
5. the descriptions miss out important aspects of Jung's theory (part 1: Spoto's critique);
6. the descriptions miss out important aspects of Jung's theory (part 2: Garden's critique);
7. personality questionnaires only measure how people answer questionnaires, not how they actually behave in real life or anything that matters;
8. what the number part of MBTI results measure is at best confused and unclear;
9. the MBTI is unnecessary and just a racket for making money. The descriptions are sufficient on their own;
10. type is just like astrology.

And the queries:

1. Are some types better managers, counsellors, etc.?
2. Why is there so little research on the MBTI in the major personality journals?
3. Can I change my type?
4. How can I discover my type?
5. How easy is it to tell what type someone is?
6. How different are people of the same type?
7. How is type misused?
8. Does the MBTI work in different cultures?
9. Why can't I answer 'both' to the MBTI items when options (a) and (b) are both true?

CRITICISMS

Type and MBTI results are an insult to individuality

Variations of this criticism are that type 'puts people in boxes', labels and stereotypes, fails to do justice to the complexity and richness of human personality and diminishes our vision of who we are.

Reply

Type and MBTI results do not try to capture individuality. Rather, they offer a broad framework which helps people move towards appreciating individuality, in much the same way that the distinction between blue and black helps organize colours and 'plant' versus 'animal' helps make sense of the natural world. What type does is suggest four of the most important ways in which personalities differ: Jung's 'compass points in the wilderness of the psyche'. People are much more complicated than type but we generalize in order to understand, think and communicate.

A different kind of argument is that if we measured 20 unrelated personality characteristics on ten-point scales, the number of individual, unique sets of results would be 20 billion. Individuality in this sense is readily available. This argument applies more to type theory and the Expanded Analysis Report (EAR) of the MBTI than to the MBTI itself and may at first sight seem a bit glib, but I think it has a core of truth. At the same time, I think individuality is more than the sum of a number of characteristics; therefore the criticism too has a core of truth.

Type does carry the risk of stereotyping. However, a further aspect of the argument above is that categories are inevitable: the choice of starting afresh with each person (or each time we meet that person) is not a realistic one. As we use categories anyway – and we would be overwhelmed or silent if we did not – then respect for individuality involves finding the best categories (which is what theories try to do) and using them flexibly, tentatively and with respect. The categories – types in this case – are not the person. The preferences and types are reference points, not pigeon-holes, and can be experienced as very liberating. In this respect, they are unlike most labels. Indeed, a useful first response to someone who says type is insulting is to clarify their previous experience with labels.

Behaviour is different in different situations

The criticism here is that people behave differently in different situations. We are flexible persons, not rigid automatons, and have a rich repertoire of selves to choose from. Part of being fully human is choosing which self to be in each situation. Because there is little or no consistency in our behaviour in different (or the same) situations, personality characteristics like 'honest', 'extravert' and 'generous' are meaningless and misleading and personality measures like the MBTI are pointless.

Reply

Most people behave as if personalities exist. We choose friends and partners at least in part because they behave most of the time in certain recognizable ways. Even people who argue that personality traits do not exist probably write references using trait terms and select colleagues and others on the basis of consistencies.

Empirically, the personality versus situation controversy is now, after an enormous amount of research and argument, generally seen by psychologists as resolved. First, particular behaviours are consistent across time. For example, Epstein (1979) asked students to keep records for two weeks of how often they made phone calls, wrote letters and initiated social contacts. They were highly consistent. Second, different behaviours tend to cluster together, e.g. Small *et al.* (1983) studied adolescents on a 30-day expedition and found strong relationships between different ways of being helpful, e.g. giving information and sharing food, and between different ways of being dominant, e.g. giving instructions and being forceful. Third, situations have an effect. When we describe someone as calm, it means 'tends to be and behave more calmly than most people', not 'never gets angry'. We can predict their behaviour on average (Kenrick and Funder, 1988).

The broader the trait term, the less useful it is for predicting a specific behaviour, but the more manageable it is. The distinctions between plant and animal or black and blue have the same kind of function. Thus the preferences are a broader kind of concept than traits; they underlie clusters of traits and thus colour many aspects of each person's life. Knowing a person's preference (in the MBTI sense) we can predict much of their experience and behaviour most of the time.

Other complexities in the relationship between situations and personality have also been clarified. For example, people actively seek out situations which are compatible with their personalities and actively avoid those which are not. Traits influence behaviour only or most in relevant situations. A person's traits can affect a situation. Traits in general are expressed in some situations more easily than others, e.g. going on a picnic as opposed to watching a film. Goals or motives may be more important consistencies than behaviour (Kenrick and Funder, 1988).

Kenrick and Funder (1988) provide a sophisticated overview of most of the lessons learned about personality and its assessment from the personality versus situation debate. In their view the research clearly indicates that accurate judgements of personality (and therefore accurate predictions of a person's behaviour throughout their life) are more likely if made by someone who knows the person well, if they're based on several sets of observations by several people and the observations are of behaviours which can be observed and which are relevant to the quality being judged (Kenrick and Funder, 1988, p. 31).

Conversely, accuracy is more difficult to achieve in constrained situations, like funerals and job interviews, or when a single behaviour is the basis for a prediction. I agree with Kenrick and Funder that the outcomes of the long debate on personality versus situation are only obvious with hindsight. Indeed, it is easy to think of situations where they are not acted on: e.g. any first impression, even by an 'expert judge' (see Chapter 6).

The personality versus situation data also offer a quite different 'lesson': that we sometimes underestimate the power of situations. However, although our behaviour varies according to situations (or we would be rigid and robotlike) we are the same person in those situations, with recognizable patterns and themes of experience or behaviour (or we would feel depersonalized and empty).

I think personality traits are now clearly established as real (Funder, 1991) and that there is considerable agreement on which are the most important (Goldberg, 1993; Bayne, 1994).

The descriptions are too vague and general

The idea behind this criticism is that the type descriptions are sufficiently general for most people to see themselves in most or at least several of them.

Reply

The studies discussed in the next reply are clear evidence against this criticism. However, there is a class of vague personality descriptions, called Barnum statements, which are also relevant.

Research on Barnum statements began with Forer (1949). He first collected several sentences describing personality, mostly from a news-stand astrology book. Examples are in Table 5.1. His experimental design, and the basis of most studies of Barnum statements since, was as follows:

1. A group of subjects completes a personality test.
2. After time for scoring the tests, each subject is given an identical copy of a personality analysis, i.e. a 'fake' sketch, consisting of Barnum personality statements.
3. Without conferring or seeing each other's analyses, the subjects rate the accuracy of their own analysis and the effectiveness of the test.

The main finding (Furnham and Schofield, 1987) is that the Barnum statements are rated by most of the subjects as accurate and the personality tests given are rated as effective. For example, 90% of Stagner's (1958) sample of 68 personnel managers rated the sketches as 'amazingly accurate' or 'rather good'. Including 'genuine' statements (i.e. from a personality test) did not reduce

Table 5.1: Barnum statements (with instructions) (from Forer, 1949)

Personality interpretation

Please consider each of the following statements and mark it as *True* (✔) about yourself, *False* (x) or *?*.

You have a great need for people to like and admire you.

You have a tendency to be critical of yourself.

You have a great deal of unused capacity which you have not turned to your advantage.

While you have some personality weaknesses, you are generally able to compensate for them.

Your sexual adjustment has presented problems for you.

Disciplined and self-controlled outside, you tend to worry and be insecure inside.

At times you have serious doubts as to whether you have made the right decision or done the right thing.

You prefer a certain amount of change and variety and become dissatisfied when hemmed in by restrictions and limitations.

You pride yourself as an independent thinker and do not accept others' statements without satisfactory proof.

You have found it unwise to be frank in revealing yourself to others.

At times you are extraverted, affable, sociable, while at other times you are introverted, wary, reserved.

Some of your aspirations tend to be pretty unrealistic.

Security is one of your major goals in life.

You feel great sometimes, other times like hiding away.

You need close relationships but at the same time hate being restricted by them.

You are trying to go the way you want to go and are beginning to succeed.

1. Please rate the interpretation of your personality on the following scale:

   Excellent   Good   Average   Poor   Very Poor

2. How helpful do you find the description?

---

subjects' acceptance. Thus Hampson *et al.* (1978) asked for ratings of 'genuine' statements (from each subject's 16 PF scores) as well as Barnum statements. All the statements were rated as accurate. O'Dell (1972) compared responses to three personality sketches – 16 PF, fake and one containing 'as much clinical jargon as possible'. The fake sketch, composed of Barnum statements, was rated the most accurate.

One interpretation of this clear and consistent finding is that people are gullible about their own personalities. An alternative view is that the statements actually **are** accurate, though in a general sense only. Either way, when trying to distinguish one person from another they are, at best, a waste of time. Worse, they may be a factor in increasing the confidence of judgements made about self and others. Apart from taking up space, they can reduce appropriate doubt and give a misplaced sense of confidence. The question for the MBTI descriptions is how many Barnum statements they contain. There are not enough to prevent the descriptions being differentially valid but if there are any Barnum statements they should of course be replaced.

Some of the Barnum statements seem to work through being vague, others through flattery. A strategy for informally detecting them is to ask 'Is this description true of a number of people of different types?' or 'Is this true of two or three people I know, as well as me?'. The more formal method is Forer's, but it may be unnecessarily elaborate. It is surprising that new Barnum statements haven't been tested. Presumably it's because interest has been in the phenomenon rather than the content. I think their content has implications for personality, at least at the level of self-concept, and that new ones are worth testing. Table 5.2 contains some suggestions.

Table 5.2: Some possible Barnum statements

You are trying to go the way you want to go and are beginning to succeed.
A lot of your difficulties are caused by the extraordinary demands you make on yourself.
There's a lot of hurt underneath your anger.
There's a lot of anger underneath your pain.

The MBTI Report Form descriptions are too positive

A colleague described the MBTI Report Form descriptions (see Table 3.1) as 'vignettes of unrelenting virtue'. He meant they were too good to be true, that positive statements are flattering and that perhaps most people agree with them for this reason, rather than because they are accurate.

Reply

First, the descriptions are not meant to capture the whole of personality but rather some broad themes. Second, there is the 'twist' in some type descriptions (Chapters 1, 7 and 9) so they are not always relentlessly positive. Third, the positive quality of the Report Form descriptions is very valuable for its unthreatening and constructive effect (generally speaking) when the topic – oneself – is sensitive.

There is also considerable evidence that the descriptions are accurate (reviewed in Chapters 2 and 3), so their positive tone is not a problem in this respect. Thus people select the descriptions of their own type much more often than those of similar types or the opposite types (Carskadon, 1982; Carskadon and Cook, 1982). Carskadon (1982) gave the MBTI to 118 introductory psychology students. A week later, he gave each student one-page descriptions of five different types in random order:

1. their MBTI type;
2. their type if the lowest scoring preference was reversed;
3. their type if EI and JP were reversed;
4. their type if SN and TF were reversed;
5. the opposite type to their MBTI type.

The students were asked to rank order the five descriptions and rate their accuracy.

The main result was that 35% of the students ranked the description based on their MBTI results as the most accurate and 31% the description with their lowest scoring preference reversed. Only 4% chose the opposite description. Given the youth of the participants and the lack of other information about type, e.g. exercises and fuller descriptions, this result is a strong counter to the 'too positive and too vague' criticisms.

Carskadon (1982) also asked the students to predict their MBTI results for each preference from 'short descriptions' of them. They were able to do this with a good degree of accuracy for all the preferences: for EI (68%), SN (66%), TF (63%) and JP (72%).

Carskadon and Cook (1982) replicated this study with 118 introductory psychology students. This time four descriptions were used and the gap was eight weeks. The missing description, surprisingly, was the one for the lowest scoring preference reversed. Fifty per cent chose their MBTI description and 10% the opposite description. This is statistically and practically significant and confirmed the strong support for the perceived accuracy of the basic descriptions.

The two studies raise other questions, e.g. do some of the types find their descriptions more accurate than other types find theirs? If so, are they right? (As Carskadon and Cook point out, some types are predicted to be more critical.) Can the descriptions be improved? And what happens when the MBTI results are verified more thoroughly?

Walck (1992a) studied the last of these questions. The MBTI was completed by 256 undergraduates who were studying mainly business and engineering. They verified their results in a variety of ways: with a student counsellor, through writing an essay explaining their choice of true type, giving examples from their own experience, speculating about the type of a close friend or relative, through access to various handouts and books on type and through opportunities for discussion and a lecture on type theory.

Using the participant's final choice of type after this thorough (though quite short-term) verification, 75% of them agreed with their MBTI type and none changed either three or four of the MBTI preferences (21% changed one and only 4% two).

Walck also reported that 81% of the changes were made on preferences that were low (i.e. an MBTI number score of 1–9). Out of a possible total of 1012 preference scores, 57 slight preferences were changed and 13 moderate or clear preferences (moderate is defined as a score of 11–19). The proportion of moderate or clear MBTI preferences that were changed after Walck's procedure was therefore negligible.

Walck remarks that Hammer and Yeakley's (1987) interview method of verifying MBTI results may have a similar impact. If so, the impact would be achieved much more economically than in her verification procedure. In the interviews, participants were 'asked to discuss their true preferences. In all cases a consensus was reached between the respondent and the interviewer as to the true type of the respondent' (p.52). No other information was given. Hammer and Yeakley's 120 participants were older (80% between 35 and 55) than Walck's student sample and 85% agreed with their MBTI results. The 18 disagreements with MBTI results were all with slight preferences. The authors, despite this strong support for the MBTI's validity, recommend that 'Ideally, multiple measures of type (observation, interviews, indicator results) should converge over a period of time before one is confident that true type has been accurately estimated' (p.55). Walck and I would include exercises, consultation and reading under the general term 'observation' (see Chapter 2, pp. 19–20).

Other studies have also investigated the perceived accuracy of the descriptions, comparing Myers' and Keirsey's descriptions. For example, McCarley and Carskadon (1986) asked three main questions:

1. Which elements are most accurate?
2. Should the type descriptions be different for males and females?
3. Do the type descriptions stereotype sensing types?

The Myers descriptions used were those in Myers (1976) and (1980), longer therefore than those in the Report Form (Table 3.1). A large number of students (352 males and 257 females) completed the MBTI as part of their psychology course. All types (in terms of their MBTI results) were represented, with INFJs and ENTJs the least common (15 students or 2.5% of each) and ISTJs the most (70 or 11.5%). These proportions are quite surprising in a psychology class, which is normally dominated by Ns and NFs (e.g, Table 3.8). In terms of temperaments, there were 39% SJs, 26% SPs, 19% NFs and 15% NTs: much more like the general USA population than I'd expect but it was an introductory class, as the number of students implies.

The 609 participants rated each statement of the Myers and Keirsey descriptions of their own MBTI type for accuracy. Ideally, perhaps, all participants would have rated all 16 descriptions but the task would have been enormous. As it is, the results are very lengthy. For example, the ISTJ table contains two statements rated high, 22 relatively high, four relatively low and two very low.

Table 5.3 lists the top rated element by each type. Are they Barnum statements as discussed in the last section? Perhaps a fairer question would be 'Are they Barnum statements in context?' because the descriptions are a series of statements some of which modify others. For example, the top INFJ statement is 'I want to see my ideas worked out in practice, accepted and applied' which, in isolation, sounds rather unlike INFJs. However, the second most highly rated statement was 'I have a strong drive to contribute to the welfare of others and genuinely enjoy helping my fellow human', which suggests the kind of idea involved.

Table 5.3 The element of the Myers and Keirsey descriptions rated most highly by each type (modified from McCarley and Carskadon 1986)

ISTJ	When I give my word, I give my honour.
ISFJ	I am very dependable.
INFJ	I want to see my ideas worked out in practice, accepted and applied.
INTJ	I look to the future rather than the past.
ISTP	I am fond of sports and outdoors.
ISFP	I love having the freedom to do whatever I please.
INFP	I tend to care very deeply about a few special persons or about a cause.
INTP	I prize intelligence in myself and others.
ESTP	I get more from first-hand experience than from study.
ESFP	I enjoy the good things in life: dress, food, physical comfort and happy times.
ENFP	I possess a wide range and variety of feelings.
ENTP	I value adaptability and innovation (trying new things).
ESTJ	I like to see things done correctly.
ESFJ	I am loyal to persons, institutions and causes that I respect.
ENFJ	As ESFJ
ENTJ	I know how to be tough when the situation calls for toughness.

McCarley and Carskadon emphasize caution in interpreting their results and the need for replication. Nearly all the participants were aged between 18 and 21, when type development would generally be less advanced. That they were also students would also be likely to have an effect on ratings of some of the elements. Their general conclusions are that statements from both Myers and Keirsey were rated high and low about equally, that there were no sex differences of practical significance, that the descriptions of sensing types were not rated lower by sensing types than were those of intuitive types by intuitive types, that – in line with the other studies discussed in this section – most of the elements were rated as accurate (with the ISTP description the exception) and that there is room for improvement.

Ruhl and Rodgers (1992) also found nearly identical ratings for overall accuracy of the Myers and Keirsey descriptions. In addition, descriptions of thinking types were rated as less valid by thinking types than those of feeling types by feeling types. However, the difference was not a substantial one – though perhaps, given thinking types' tendency to be more critical, it should have been. Again undergraduate students (145, but not equally distributed by type) were the participants and unverified MBTI types were the criterion of 'true type'.

A provocative additional finding was that the Myers descriptions were rated most highly by three F types and the Keirsey descriptions by two T types and one F type. Myers was an INFP and Keirsey is an INTP. Although there were very few of some of the types, e.g. three INFJs and five ISTPs, this aspect seems worth studying further.

The descriptions miss out important aspects of Jung's theory

Part 1: Spoto's critique

Myers designed the MBTI to implement Jung's theory of type (Myers and McCaulley, 1985; Myers, 1980). However, several writers, most prominently McCrae and Costa (1989), Spoto (1989, 1993) and Garden (1991), have criticized the MBTI for distorting and contradicting Jung's ideas. Spoto (1993) put this point differently when he said the MBTI has 'broken away from Jung' and is developing independently.

Spoto's (1989, 1993) argument is based on the assumption that the unconscious is 'always encroaching' and much more influential than recognized in most writings about the MBTI. By 'unconscious' he means in part the idea that 'life is made up everywhere of pairs of opposites which are at once irreconcilable as well as inseparable' (1989, p. 28). Applying this idea to extraversion–introversion, this means that 'the extraversion–introversion *polarity* is the issue for Jung, not simply extraverting or introverting' (p. 29). On this view, extraverts, for example, are introverted at the unconscious level and this 'fact', and the balance between the conscious and unconscious, affects how a person behaves as much as their conscious extraversion does.

Spoto (1989) concludes that 'Because the unconscious is constantly a factor and condition of the individual's psychological type, it is much more difficult to determine an individual's type than one might believe or than typological tests may indicate' (p. 121). And towards the end of his book he becomes increasingly scornful. First, a cautiously phrased remark: 'In effect, Jungian typology as incarnated in the MBTI may be trying to say too much about consciousness at the expense of the unconscious' (p. 133). Second, he suggests that Kroeger and Hirsh offer a 'tidy and palatable rendition' of Jung's typology, which he compares to 'the fisherman calmly fishing for minnows from atop the back of a whale' (p. 134). In other words, Kroeger and others are naively ignoring the 'whale' of the Jungian unconscious. At the same time, Spoto states that 'the MBTI is very helpful on problems relating to ego-consciousness and the development of the conscious side of one's psychological type' (p. 142). But his main criticism stands: as he put it in his 1993 Conference Address, 'You need a reverence for the unconscious to work well with type'.

Reply

The evidence against Spoto's criticism of the MBTI is summarized in Chapter 2, on validity, and Chapter 6, on observing type accurately. Since in practice we observe type fairly accurately, it follows that the unconscious is less influential than Spoto thinks and it is possible to work well with type without revering the unconscious. Indeed, in its Jungian sense, the unconscious may not even be a useful concept. Contemporary psychology tends to see the unconscious as performing more routine activities, like driving (Loftus and Klinger, 1992) – a radically different view from Spoto's.

I see the 'unconscious' as much less influential than Spoto does, as more like a companion and an imp than a vast unknown, 'like an ocean' (Spoto, 1993). My unconscious, as far as I can tell, plays a valuable but occasional part in my life; I'm comfortable thinking of myself as an MBTI practitioner, not a Jungian, and seeing the difference between the two theories as a strength, not a problem.

Spoto's criticism of the MBTI and of type theory as presented by Kroeger, Hirsh and in this book is related to a broader controversy within psychology: when is the conscious part of personality the most influential and when the unconscious, or, as the title of a recent review put it: 'Is the unconscious smart or dumb?' (Loftus and Klinger, 1992). On the 'conscious' side of the controversy there are Allport (e.g. 1961a) and most modern psychologists and on the 'unconscious' side, Freud, Jung and others. Freud's view was that under the surface we seethe with lust and rage and are amoral and irrational. Therefore we do things for reasons we don't understand (though we may well think we understand). Jung saw the unconscious as more complicated: as containing archetypes (see Rytting (1990) for an empirical and clear perspective), creative energies and (as noted above) complementary qualities to conscious ones, as well as lust and rage.

The controversy is about the relative importance of unconscious and conscious motives in personality. Imagine you could only ask a single question to understand someone's personality and suppose you had to choose between 'What types of fantasies do you have?' and 'What do you want to be doing five years from now?' (Allport, 1961a, p. 224). The first emphasizes unconscious influences, the second conscious purposes. Allport's view was that **neurotic** behaviour is indeed often due to unconscious motives and conflict, but that most people are relatively well integrated and balanced and therefore mainly influenced by conscious purposes. Similarly, some of the defence mechanisms identified by Freud are used quite widely, but 'Normal persons employ them more sparingly and often with a corrective measure of self-insight and humour' (Allport, 1961a, p. 164). McCrae and Costa's view (in press) is very similar: 'Trait psychologists who rely on self-report methods generally assume that the self-concept is reasonably accurate, although they acknowledge that it may sometimes be distorted'.

Allport (1961a) discusses the idea of 'the mature personality' along similar lines, surveying a wide range of theories: unity of personality and accurate perception of the world and self are recurring themes (pp. 277ff). The key question for Spoto's criticism of the MBTI then echoes the question about the incidence of actualization of the real self discussed in Chapter 1. Are most people (a) largely unaware of their real motives, driven primarily by a dynamic unconscious, or (b) relatively self-aware and, to use another of Allport's terms, 'all of a piece'? Jung's theory of psychological type, and therefore Spoto, assumes (a) to be the case; I have argued for (b) and Myers' theory of type.

Part 2: Garden's critique

Garden (1991) criticized the MBTI on similar grounds to Spoto, but focused on four issues in Myers' theory. The first two issues are quite technical but both are examples of Jung's theory stating one view and Myers another.

Issues 1 and 2

'Does the JP dimension determine the extraverted function and, hence, the dominant function?' (Garden, 1991, p. 4), and 'Is the auxiliary of an introvert, extraverted and that of an extravert, introverted? Further, is the auxiliary complementary to, or antagonistic to, the dominant?' (p. 6).

Reply

I think of J and P first as a valuable individual difference in their own right. Second, they also appear much of the time to point to the main extraverted function and therefore the dominant and auxiliary, though this idea does need to be tested more directly. However, the type descriptions embody the set of ideas which Garden criticizes and are reasonably accurate (as discussed earlier).

Issue 3

'Is everybody a type?' (p. 7)

Reply

Some people are, at the very least, hard to 'type' accurately, either by themselves or by others. Myers' theory and the MBTI seem to me able to cope with
this. However, Garden (p. 7) cites Jung as saying that an 'extensive middle
group' is 'influenced as much from within as from without', i.e. is *equally* E
and I. I disagree. Most people seem happy with the idea of being basically
either one or the other with development to varying degrees of both. And the
same holds for all the preferences.

Costa and McCrae's longitudinal research on five factor theory (e.g. McCrae,
1993) also supports the idea that everyone is a type. They found that people
answer their questionnaire similarly, and are rated by others similarly, on different occasions many years apart. Their five factors are thus highly stable (and
strongly related to the four preferences). McCrae concludes 'Barring such
events as dementia and major depressive episodes, stable individual differences
in basic personality traits are a universal part of human nature' (p. 583).

Issue 4

'Should the MBTI be used outside the context of Jungian theory?' (p. 9)

Reply

Garden sees in MBTI writings 'a concentration on the *behavioural, conscious,*
and *cognitive* aspects of Jung's theory' (p. 9) and these aspects as 'partial and
probably less important'. To me a major strength of the MBTI is this very focus
on conscious aspects, treating unconscious ones as a special case. Further, I
usually think of type development in terms of degrees of consciousness and
competence, rather than with an unconscious, psychodynamic flavour. I do not
see the conscious as the 'tip of the iceberg' (Garden, 1991, p. 10). Of course,
psychodynamic theorists can say 'Ah, but you're not **aware** ...'.

Garden further argues that ignoring the 'unconscious' aspects will cause
trouble. This too is an empirical question and a way of comparing the value of
the two theories. Meanwhile, I do not agree that 'use of the MBTI needs to take
place only within the context of the wider underlying theory from which it
sprang' (p. 13) – by which Garden means Jungian theory. The MBTI 'sprang'
from Myers and Briggs and I think it is used well with reference to Myers'
theory. Of course, it is sometimes misused too, as is Jungian theory, but that is a
different issue.

Overall, I agree with Garden (1991) that there are fundamental differences between Myers' theory and the MBTI on the one hand and Jung's theory on the other. I also found Garden's analysis of some of the issues very clear and helpful. However, I am much happier than her about the differences between the two theories and have no wish to change the MBTI or its main applications because of those differences.

A typology of positions on Myers' and Jung's theories of type may clarify their differences further:

1. preferring Myers' theory and simpler variations of it, e.g. Keirsey, to Jung's theory and seeing Jung as historically important and/or a rich source of hypotheses but in either case as not central;
2. wishing to supplement – on special occasions or routinely – the MBTI with other measures: the Expanded Analysis Report, the Type Differentiation Indicator, the Lewis and Lowe (1992) measure and/or the Cambridge Type Inventory (Rawling, 1994);
3. preferring Jung's theory, seeing Myers and the MBTI as a 'wrong turning' and therefore wishing to replace the MBTI with another measure;
4. seeing Myers and the MBTI as only a partial expression of Jung's richer approach, but liking them both.

I place myself in (1) with occasional leanings towards (2). However, if another measure of type or another theory (Jung's or someone else's) were shown to be as positive and unthreatening to use as the MBTI and/or more valid, that would make a radical difference.

At present, Myers' theory and the MBTI are far better supported empirically than Jungian theory, though still of course with much to clarify, test and refine. In particular, as Garden points out, much of the evidence for the validity of the MBTI supports it as a measure of four of the five main individual differences in personality rather than of types. Therefore, we need to clarify and test structural and dynamic aspects of Myers' theory (and Jung's). This issue is discussed in Chapter 3.

Personality questionnaires only measure how people answer questionnaires, not how they actually behave in real life

This criticism can be interpreted in two related ways: that personality questionnaires are too simple and that they are easy to fake. Consider an MBTI item like 'At parties, do you (a) Sometimes get bored, (b) Always have fun?'. The only reasonable literal answer for most people would be 'It depends' or 'Both'. If you answer it in the spirit in which it's asked, i.e. which is **more** true of you, generally speaking?, then you would need to search through your memory, define 'fun', take your self-concept into account (e.g. 'I'm never bored'), decide and respond honestly on the answer sheet. There are therefore lots of opportunities for error. (In an item that asks you to compare yourself with others, there is even more scope for error: for example, no-one has access to a random sample

of people in a random sample of situations to compare themselves with.) There
are also lots of reasons to fake, especially if there is something to gain, e.g. a
job or the approval of whoever sees the results.

Reply

Responses to personality questionnaires can be interpreted as indications or estimates of what the person is really like, or of the person's self-concept, or as
self-presentations. Costa and McCrae (1992) suggest that all three interpretations are correct to some extent. In terms of the theories discussed in Chapter 1,
all three will be more consistent with each other – more 'all of a piece' – in
some people than in others (see Fig. 1.1).

 In practice, perhaps surprisingly, the major personality questionnaires work
fairly well as measures of what the person is really like. Even in situations
where faking would be rewarded, people tend not to fake (e.g. Costa and
McCrae, 1992). The criticism echoes the Spoto and Garden critiques discussed
above, with their distrust of self-report. Costa and McCrae's measure of the Big
Five factors uses self-report for several reasons. First, there is in their view
'substantial evidence' that self-reports are trustworthy, e.g. other people agree
with them. Second, subtle items are less valid in practice. Third, they do not
regard the use of measures 'designed to outwit or entrap the respondent' (p. 8)
as contributing to trust and rapport. They recognize that self-reports are not
trustworthy sometimes – but that was a major reason for developing an observer
form of their measure. Consistent with Kenrick and Funder (1988), they recommend obtaining ratings from knowledgeable informants, e.g. spouses, parents,
when it seems appropriate.

**What the number part of MBTI results measures is at best confused and
unclear**

Reply

This is a complicated issue. The MBTI *Manual* (Myers and McCaulley, 1985)
is unclear about it and some of the main research studies interpret the number
results wrongly – at least, they do if the 'official' interpretation is true. This is
that the number results only measure how clearly the person has voted; they do
not measure how much of the preference someone has, how good they are at it,
or type development.

 For example, compare two sets of MBTI results for thinking versus feeling.
Person A's result is T35 F3 and Person B's T3 F35. On the 'clarity of vote'
interpretation we cannot say with any validity that A is more highly developed
in thinking than B. Nor can we say that A is more highly developed in thinking
than in feeling.

There is a problem here, though: the number results do make a difference to behaviour. This is illustrated by the relationships between MBTI results expressed as continuous dimensions rather than types and other personality dimensions (e.g. the Big Five, as discussed earlier). It is also illustrated, often, in workshops when groups representing each preference are formed on the basis of the number results – high scores on T in one group for example, medium to low scores on T in another and so on. This suggests that on average the number results measure more than clarity of voting, but it says nothing about either (a) whether or not they measure development or skill or (b) how useful they are for individual interpretation.

One source of confusion is that 'high' results are described as 'clear' and 'strong'. This implies 'vague' and 'weak' for low number results and detracts from the MBTI's positive and relatively unthreatening tone. A second source of confusion – perhaps because of the seductiveness of numbers – is the MBTI *Manual*. It states, for example, that 'Scores were designed to show the direction of a preference, not its intensity' (Myers and McCaulley, 1985, p. 58) – that's the clarity of voting interpretation – but also that 'The characteristics associated with a preference are often less apparent when the numerical portion of the preference score is low' (p. 3). The key word here is 'often'. Does it mean more than chance? Sufficiently more than chance to be a useful clue in individual interpretations? Either way, the two statements seem to contradict each other.

Similarly, the *Manual* states that 'It is sometimes useful to compare scores for the dominant and auxiliary. According to theory, the dominant will show a clearer preference than will the auxiliary' (p. 58). Yet the data quoted in the *Manual* (p. 58) show clearly that dominants have a higher number score only about half the time, i.e. chance. A chance relationship does not justify the use of the numbers as an 'alert' or a 'clinical sign' (p. 58).

McCrae and Costa (1989) replicated the finding that dominant functions do not have higher number scores than auxiliaries and interpreted it as evidence against the MBTI as a measure of dominant and auxiliary functions and against the idea that these are useful concepts. They are right if the number scores measure development, but not if they measure clarity of vote.

I'm left with the related facts that:

1. the MBTI scales function well as trait measures, but not so well as to justify use of the numbers in any rigorous way in individual interpretations of MBTI results – though they do seem fairly consistently to make a difference in exercises and research;
2. low numbers (under ten) tend to be associated with misclassification (Hammer and Yeakley, 1987; Kummerow, 1988) but many people with low scores are nevertheless sure about their preference;
3. people, even experienced MBTI practitioners, say things like 'I've got 0 for sensing; that means I haven't got any at all' or 'I've scored three more than last time for thinking; I'm improving', which are not justified;

4. that the Expanded Analysis Report (EAR) of the MBTI uses all the MBTI items and treats the preferences as traits: more confusion! It seems that something has to change.

My current resolution is to distinguish between (1) behaving more in the ways indicated by the number part of the results and (2) behaving in more developed and skilful ways. The numbers measure (1) more than (2), e.g. someone who scores T43 probably makes most decisions logically but the logic may or may not be subtle, insightful or consistent. But primarily I try to ignore the numbers for most purposes, especially in verifying an individual's MBTI results. This is because they are so seductive. They are also inconsistent with the MBTI as a categorizing indicator. If there were, say, ten preferences to verify, I think there would be more point in using the numbers to suggest which to spend most time on, but four preferences scores are manageable.

The MBTI is unnecessary and just a racket for making money. The descriptions are sufficient on their own

This criticism accuses the MBTI of being a 'con trick', more show than substance and a lot more complicated than necessary. It is reminiscent of Shaw's remark about the professions being a conspiracy against the laity.

Reply

Again my answer is partly an empirical one. In practice, people actually are more accurate, more quickly, about their types when they start from an MBTI result than from the Report Form or other descriptions. There are too many types to hold in mind and people are generally better at seeing consistencies in other people whom they know quite well than in themselves. Perhaps we have too much information about ourselves.

An interview with a skilled interviewer who is also knowledgeable about type would probably end with the same result as the MBTI (and use similar questions to the items) but at much greater expense. Similarly, a person's behaviour could be observed for a few days, preferably in a wide range of situations. But it is obviously expensive to do this and would also lack the very careful calculations which are part of designing a formal, properly constructed psychometric test.

Type is just like astrology

This criticism is sometimes stated as a compliment.

Reply

Type is like astrology in some respects but not, on current evidence, in the most important ones of rationale and validity. The aims of the two theories and measures are the same and both have a largely positive, constructive tone and a flexible, complicated view of personality. Both are also misrepresented on occasion. Moreover, descriptions based on an astrological chart are often individual, not just Barnum-like (as discussed earlier in this chapter). The problem with astrology is that there have been several thousand studies of it and none so far has produced good evidence of any accuracy about individual personalities. Other studies, like those in which the researcher deliberately gave the wrong descriptions to people who were then satisfied, are strong evidence against astrology's validity (see, for example, Dean, 1986–7).

CONCLUSIONS

1. Each of us is a particular psychological type, but in an individual and unique way. Type descriptions are a step towards understanding individuality rather than an attempt to capture it.
2. Behaviour is influenced both by situations and by personality characteristics. Personality characteristics are stable across situations and over time.
3. MBTI descriptions are not too positive or too vague and general.
4. Myers herself saw the MBTI as applying Jung's theory but I agree with Spoto and Garden that in some respects it does not. I think Myers undervalued her own contribution in selecting some of Jung's ideas and clarifying and developing them. The differences between Myers' theory and Jung's are therefore a strength, not a problem.

QUERIES

Are some types better managers, counsellors, etc.?

According to type theory, some types are better **on average** at some activities, but if you are selecting someone for a job, it would be more effective and ethical to select on the basis of type development. An advertisement for an organizational psychologist which stated 'ESTJs and people who do not know what that means need not apply' was a misuse of type theory, because the first part of the criterion discriminates unfairly against ESTJs. The best candidate might be any of the types, including ESTJ. If the job required primarily 'N' and 'F' skills, then a particular ESTJ might have developed those skills more than any of the other candidates, including those whose type actually includes 'N' and 'F'. Depending on the job, asking for knowledge of psychological type theory is a much more defensible criterion!

Moreover, in many jobs, it is possible to achieve the same level of performance in different ways or to be excellent at some elements of the job and adequate in others. This issue is discussed further in Chapter 9.

Why is there so little research on the MBTI in the major personality journals?

Similarly, the MBTI is not mentioned, or only touched on, in textbooks of psychology and even in textbooks of personality theories. Given the large number of such texts and the widespread use of the MBTI, this is surprising. I think it is partly a matter of fashion: research topics come and go (and sometimes return under another name). Other probable factors are that there are many worthwhile questions to research, that 'type' is a dubious word – guilt by association with 'fringe' techniques – and suspicion of commercial success and popularity. The few studies that have been published in the major journals, e.g. Carlson and Levy (1973), Hicks (1984), have been of high quality. It might be an interesting question to study formally. I suspect that a major factor is that the greatest use is by applied psychologists who generally do not do research that is acceptable to major journals. There are a lot of publications on the MBTI (Carlson (1985) located over 700, so there must be 1000s now) though mainly on applications rather than empirical research.

Can I change my type?

It depends what you mean by 'type' and 'change'. The theory says that each of us is her or his true type throughout life. You can of course change your MBTI type by answering the questions differently. You can also change in the sense of developing each preference (see Chapter 4).

How can I discover my type?

Generally, the best method is to take the MBTI and verify the results carefully, taking as much time as you need. Guidelines for checking MBTI results or provisional types from any source are given at the beginning of Chapter 2. The quickest way for some people is to ask someone who (a) knows them well and (b) knows type theory.

How easy is it to tell what type someone is?

Mistakes are easily made, however striking the evidence appears to be, because the person you are judging may have developed any of the preferences and, when observed, be using them. In practice, though, accurate judgements can be made because people generally do behave in tune with their types. Ways of increasing the likelihood of accurate judgements are discussed in Chapter 6.

How different are people of the same type?

They can be extremely different, while still having something important in common. Table 1.2 lists some of the factors involved.

Loan Receipt
Liverpool John Moores University
Learning and Information Services

Borrower ID: 21111121746119
Loan Date: 06/02/2008
Loan Time: 11:05 pm

The Myers-Briggs type indicator :
31111007011511

Due Date: 07/02/2008 23:59

The Myers-Briggs type indicator :
31111007011537
Due Date: 07/02/2008 23:59

Please keep your receipt
in case of dispute

How is type misused?

The main ways are as stereotypes – blatant as in 'INTJs don't care' and more subtle as in assuming the SJs in a team will do the administration; using the number part of MBTI results as measures of skill or type development; using MBTI results **on their own** for selection (see Chapter 9); treating MBTI results as true results, rather than verifying them; and expecting people to change their type – for example, Heavrin (1992) described how a group of executives were told by their boss that they had six months to 'become ENFJs' – their company's 'designated management type' (p.17). Such a policy turns the MBTI on its head: it is intended to help people **value** differences.

Does the MBTI work in different cultures?

The MBTI has been translated into over 20 languages so far, including French (Casas, 1990) and Korean (Sim and Kim, 1993). All cultures tested have included all 16 types, confirming the universality of type. However, proportions may be different. For example, compared with the USA, there may be more Thinking types in China (Williams *et al.*, 1992) and more Introverts in the UK (Table 3.4). However, the only country for which we have a reasonable sample of the general population so far is the USA (Table 3.2).

Why isn't there a third answer, for 'both', to the MBTI questions?

People sometimes find the MBTI frustrating because, unlike most personality questionnaires, it asks for a choice between two opposites. The reason is consistent with the theory: it assumes that people use all the preferences but prefer one from each pair and that MBTI results indicate those preferences. Perhaps the instructions could spell this out more clearly. Indeed, I quite often ask people to do the handedness exercise (see Table 1.2) before they complete the MBTI.

For other questions and answers on type and the MBTI, see Jeffries (1991) and part of Chapter 1 in Lawrence (1993).

<table>
<tr><td>

6

</td><td>

Observing type accurately: obstacles and strategies

</td></tr>
</table>

In many occupations, accurate observation of clients' or patients' personalities is part of being an effective practitioner. Accuracy is obviously helpful, too, in understanding friends, partners, children and colleagues. Ideally, verified MBTI results would be available, but in reality accuracy often needs to be achieved without using a formal personality measure like the MBTI. The observer may not be qualified to use the MBTI, the other person may not want to complete it or it may just not seem appropriate or justified.

This chapter is in four sections. First, type theory can be interpreted as suggesting three obstacles to accuracy: the difference between preference and behaviour, the idea that introverted functions are less visible, and type development. Each obstacle is briefly discussed. Second, seven obstacles to accuracy derived from research and theory on forming impressions are also discussed. However, third, recent research suggests that despite all these obstacles we generally observe personality – and, by implication, type – fairly accurately. This research also clarifies the factors related to accuracy and inaccuracy. And, fourth, I discuss strategies for counteracting the obstacles and biases and therefore, in principle, observing type more accurately or, at the least, knowing which observations are most likely to be inaccurate.

THREE OBSTACLES SUGGESTED BY TYPE THEORY

Preferences and behaviour

Preferences cannot be observed directly, however much it feels as if that is what we do. We cannot even glimpse them. At best we see cues or clues and these can be very ambiguous and subtle. For example, Kroeger and Thuesen (1988, p. 131) suggest that some thinking women (i.e. against the Western cultural stereotype) and some feeling men (also against the Western stereotype) behave in a compensatory way, respectively ultrafeminine and ultramacho, while most thinking women and men generally behave in thinking ways (sometimes very macho), and most feeling men and women generally behave in feeling ways (sometimes very feminine). The problem is, given compensatory behaviour, how can accurate observations of thinking women and feeling men be made? It begins to look dangerously as if type theory could be used to 'explain' every-thing – and therefore nothing in a predictive way – and thus to resemble the fairytale, non-scientific aspects of psychoanalysis and astrology.

Type theory avoids the 'explain everything' problem by stating that most people behave most of the time in ways that correspond with their type. Therefore, they provide valid cues for those observers who (a) know what the cues are, (b) gather enough of them and (c) avoid the biases sufficiently. Ultramasculine males and ultrafeminine females are in this view treated as special cases and even then may provide valid cues, however subtle, to their true preferences.

Some preferences are less visible

A second theoretical problem in observing type is that, as part of what 'type' means, some of the preferences are less visible than others. The most important preferences in this respect are the dominant function in most introverts and the auxiliary in most extraverts. More subtly, they may be particularly hard to observe when they are perceiving functions, because the process of taking in information is less visible than the effects of the resulting decisions. The domi-nant sensing function in ISTJs, for example, should be among the least observ-able preferences if this view is correct. Thorne and Gough's (1991) research (see Chapters 2 and 3) showed more agreement between type theory and observers' judgements of extraverts than for their judgements of introverts.

I think type theory is overstated here, though still making a very useful point and indeed one which helps make the theory a type rather than a trait theory. Although introverted dominant functions do seem to be kept 'inside' most of the time, they nevertheless affect characteristic behaviour too, i.e. not just on special occasions. INFPs, for example, as a group share certain behaviours with INFJs as a group because of their shared feeling function, e.g. gentleness. Other behaviours, which are also part of feeling, are more characteristic of one type than the other. For example, INFJs express feeling judgements more often.

Type development

The third aspect of type theory which implies a difficult task for observers is type development. According to the theory, if someone is, say, smiling, animated and at ease in a conversation then they are more likely to be extraverted or a feeling type, or both. However, there are further possibilities, each of them consistent with type theory. The person may be:

1. any of the types, with extraversion, feeling or both well developed;
2. any type, with relatively undeveloped E and F but a skilled actor;
3. making a special effort,
4. an introvert or a thinking type under great stress (see Chapter 9) and for that reason behaving uncharacteristically, 'in the grip' of their third or fourth function.

In the second, third and fourth possibilities, a skilled and knowledgeable observer would hope to notice the less authentic quality of the observed person's behaviour. In the case of good type development (the first possibility), the task would be more difficult unless the observer sees the person using their true preferences in an uncontrived way as well and can therefore make a comparative judgement.

SEVEN OBSTACLES FROM RESEARCH ON FORMING IMPRESSIONS

Research and theory on forming accurate impressions of personality suggest many further obstacles or biases (Kenrick and Funder, 1988; Dean *et al.*, 1992). Seven of these are briefly discussed:

1. the 'effort after meaning';
2. the disproportionate power of the 'vividness' effect;
3. the impact of first impressions;
4. the attractiveness of similarity;
5. the seductiveness of stereotypes;
6. the limitations of our favourite categories;
7. our tendency to underestimate the effect of situations.

Another obstacle – Barnum statements – was discussed in Chapter 5.

'Effort after meaning'

This phrase summarizes the active and creative way we observe and remember. It is a general human characteristic to look for meaning, to misinterpret sometimes and to fail to notice alternative interpretations. Figure 6.1 can be interpreted in more than one way. This bias is partly because in real life there is so much information that we have to be selective (see most introductory psychology textbooks for other examples, e.g. the Necker Cube, the Old Woman/Young Woman). Figure 6.2 illustrates the 'added meaning' part of perception: the black blob in the middle usually looks friendly or sad depending on which 'face' the observer is looking at.

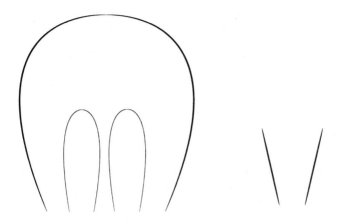

Figure 6.1 Ambiguous picture (1).

Figure 6.2 Ambiguous picture (2).

The 'vividness' effect

Part of our effort after meaning is that we look for things that go together, i.e. correlations. Any theory suggests which things go together, e.g. SJs and responsibility. However, generally we are not very skilful at detecting correlations; we tend to exaggerate the size of real correlations, make up correlations and miss correlations that actually exist (Dean *et al.*, 1992).

Table 6.1 is an example of the 'vividness' effect or bias, which is part of this lack of skill with correlations. The effect is that we tend to notice unusual events. If INFPs are unusual (which they are in some circles) and if snub noses are too, then when the two occur together it is particularly memorable. Any two characteristics would do for this example, e.g. red hair and a hot temper, Virgos and being in the acting profession. The bias arises when the observer remembers only or mainly those times she or he sees an example of the cell with ten cases in it (an INFP with a snub nose), when all four cells are relevant to the statement 'INFPs have snub noses'. (If the data in Table 6.1 are true they do not have snub noses more often than any other type. As far as I know no-one has tested the idea, but it is not completely absurd (Berry and Finch Wero, 1993).

Table: 6.1 Type and shape of nose (fictitious data)

	INFPs	Others
Snub noses	10	90
Other noses	90	900

The cell with 900 cases in it is particularly difficult to take into account in informal, everyday observations because it is not memorable and does not seem relevant to the proposed relationship. However, all four cells are actually crucial to its truth or otherwise and therefore to its usefulness as a clue to type. One other point about Table 6.1: each of the cells can be a problem. For example, in the search for proof, it is tempting to say that this person does not have a snub nose so probably is not really an INFP, thus reducing the cell with 90 in it to 89.

Another example of the vividness bias may be helpful. Suppose a consumer report based on 1000 washing machines says that brand X is the most reliable, but you know someone who owns one and it keeps going wrong. Assuming you trust the report and value reliability above other qualities, it is rational to buy brand X. But for many people the vividness of the single personal example will outweigh the much more solid data from the consumer report (Dean *et al.*, 1992).

First impressions

First impressions are very quick, almost automatic and often very rich. (Type theory implies that Ns form more complex ones, more quickly and with less awareness of cues than Ss.) Allport (1961a) recommends glancing at someone on a train, etc., closing your eyes and examining your impression. The disproportionate power of first impressions is that we tend to see them as the real person and interpret any later information which is discrepant as uncharacteristic (at least for a while!). For example, Clive seemed a friendly person (first meeting) but tired today (second meeting) or, if the two pieces of evidence were reversed, Clive seemed unfriendly (first meeting) but in an unusually good mood today (second meeting). For accuracy, the two observations should of course be weighted equally.

Similarity

This bias suggests that we observe a similarity (small or large) in another person and then tend to assume both that they are like us in other ways too **and** that we will like them and they will like us.

Stereotypes

Stereotypes are a misuse of categories. They are seductive because they are inevitable – we categorize as part of the way we observe – and because they are comforting. They too are part of our need to 'make sense' of the world.

Favourite terms

Everyone has favourite concepts for describing other people. They are an obstacle to accuracy when the person observed has important qualities which do not match our favourite terms. In contrast, a strength of type theory is that its terms are sufficiently general to apply to most and perhaps all people's personalities.

Situations

The finding here is that we tend to underestimate the effect of the situation on the person observed and to interpret their behaviour as their personality when it might be more a function of role or a reaction to other people (including ourselves!).

RECENT RESEARCH ON ACCURACY

The seven obstacles and biases outlined above are drawn from research on the process of observing other people's personalities. For many years the biases were seen as good evidence that accurate judgements are rare; in marked contrast, recent research on accuracy itself shows that our observations are generally quite accurate and it has clarified the factors related to accuracy and inaccuracy (e.g., Funder and Sneed, 1993; Kenrick and Funder, 1988). This research also shows that there is scope for improving accuracy (and most people can remember making inaccurate observations or being misjudged themselves).

The factors which affect accurate observation of personality include:

1. the person observed. Some people's personalities are more visible and some people behave more consistently than others;
2. the particular characteristic being observed, e.g. extraversion is generally more observable than, say, sense of humour;
3. the context. Informal situations allow people to express themselves more, whereas other situations are quite overpowering. First dates and selection interviews are two quite constraining contexts, though there are also individual differences in how 'authentic' people try to be in them. Type theory of course says that behaviour which is 'false' lasts only for short periods; generally, the real personality comes through in time;
4. the number of observers. Three or four observers seems to be the optimum, with larger numbers giving diminishing returns;
5. the number of observations. Single observations tend to be too risky, though of course they are often used. Looking for, say, three pieces of consistent evidence is associated with greater accuracy;
6. how well the observer knows the person observed. 'Zero acquaintance' studies (e.g. Borkenau and Liebler, 1992; Levesque and Kenny, 1993) show that the Big Five equivalents of EI and JP can be rated with much better than chance accuracy from physical cues alone, e.g. 'showy' clothes, rapid body movements and smiling for E, smiling for F, neatness and not being relaxed for J. However, all the Big Five are rated more accurately by friends and spouses than by strangers and most accurately by spouses who talk intimately to each other.

In one sense, the factors outlined above are obvious. However, they are not obvious enough to actually be used by most of us as we observe a new person (Kenrick and Funder, 1988), though they can be used if we make a deliberate attempt to do so.

STRATEGIES FOR IMPROVING ACCURACY

The seven obstacles and the recommendations drawn from research on accuracy suggest some principles and strategies for improving accuracy:

1. Look for evidence and patterns of evidence.
2. Look for evidence **against** a judgement.
3. Look for alternative interpretations of the evidence, particularly the effects of the situation.
4. Recognize the ambiguity of behaviour. The same behaviour can be evidence for more than one preference and the motive for behaving in that way may matter more than the behaviour itself.
5. Discover your own stereotypes and favourite terms and try to allow for them.
6. Compare observations with others.
7. Have a good theory or theories of personality.

The last point means knowing the theory quite well, especially which clues are most likely to be valid and which are not. Funder and Sneed (1993) made the interesting distinction between cues which are valid but not known about and those which are invalid but popular. The main category they found evidence for, however, was the first – valid cues – so their research also supports the view that people are fairly accurate observers of personality, with room for improvement.

Valid cues

All the relationships reviewed in Chapter 2, particularly those from Thorne and Gough (1991), are evidence for the construct validity of the preferences and they also suggest valid cues. Note, though, the small but useful correlations, typically about 0.20; the skilled observer looks for patterns, clusters and themes.

The remainder of this section reviews more research on cues: Thorne (1987), Seegmiller and Epperson (1987) and Ware and Rytting (1989) on some of the preferences, and Funder and Sneed (1993) and others on the factors in five factor theory which correspond to the preferences (see also the section on helping someone discover their type, in Chapter 2). The final sections review some more speculative ideas about cues for type and suggest some strategies for interviewers.

Thorne (1987) recorded ten-minute conversations of women in pairs. There were 13 conversations between introverts, 13 between extraverts and 26 between an extravert and an introvert. None of the participants had met before or knew the purpose of Thorne's research. One or two weeks later she played each participant's conversation back to her and recorded her reactions. She also asked participants to rate each other and their degree of comfort with that person.

The Es were seen as relatively outgoing, cheerful, enthusiastic and talkative and the Is as reserved, serious and shy. This is of course consistent with other research; the additional piece of information here is that Es and Is agreed on these ratings, though they disagreed on the ratings of comfort and sociability: introverts rated other Is as less sociable and comfortable than Es, while Es reported feeling comfortable with both Es and Is. As Thorne points out, Is may actually behave differently with Es than they do with Is and this was one of the main focuses of her study.

The main findings were that Es had more upbeat and expansive conversations and Is more focused and serious ones. Es seemed to have an underlying expectation that experience can and should be shared while Is tended to 'interview' Es. Es and Is also differed in specific ways which are potentially useful cues: Es gave compliments more and made more 'reaches for similarity', e.g. 'I have a pet too', while Is made more 'hedges' (using qualifying phrases like 'sort of') and expressed dissatisfaction more. These tendencies were stronger for Es with other Es and Is with other Is. In other words, the participants adapted towards a partner who differed from them on EI. In the accounts of their conversations, many of the Is felt refreshed by their E partners and some of the Es said they did not feel so pressed to say nice things and to refrain from complaining to their I partners. This seems to me a model study for its variety of question and method, and worth extending. However, it would be quite time-consuming to do.

Seegmiller and Epperson (1987) also studied language, this time as related to thinking and feeling. They found that people who prefer T use verbs like 'Think', 'Analyse', 'Decide' and 'Realize' more often and that those who prefer F use 'Feel', 'Love', 'Fear', 'Enjoy' and other emotion words more. They analysed short interviews in which the interviewees were asked to discuss a 'personally meaningful' topic for five minutes and to 'express their thoughts and feelings'. No account was taken in their analysis of direction of T or F (either extraverted or introverted) or of dominant and auxiliary, but the effect was quite a strong one. Taking the clearest 16 results on both measures (out of 39 participants altogether), nine people were classified as T on both and six as F on both, with just one T on the MBTI classified as an F on his or her language.

Ware and Rytting (1989) investigated an aspect of Js' need for structure and order in the outside world and Ps' need for flexibility. They presented photographs of the inside of students' cars to other students who had had a two-hour lecture on the MBTI and were given brief descriptions of J and P. Their accuracy was about 65%, with orderliness and fewer objects the main cue (for J). The results might have been clearer if EI had also been taken into account, but this level of accuracy is probably as much as it is reasonable to expect.

Funder and Sneed (1993) asked two questions:

1. Which behavioural cues tend to be associated with which personality characteristics, e.g. what kinds of behaviour do Es exhibit compared with Is?
2. Which behavioural cues do judges of personality actually use when forming impressions?

They argued that the answers to these two questions are not necessarily the same: people might give valid cues that are not used by observers and observers might use cues that are not valid and of course some people, in some situations, deliberately give clues which are not valid, perhaps because they want to be polite or tactful or to 'create a good impression'.

Funder and Sneed filmed randomly chosen opposite-sex pairs, who did not know each other, talking for five minutes about whatever they liked. A few weeks later, each person was filmed again with another partner they did not know. The way each of the 140 participants behaved was then categorized, using 62 statements describing a fairly general level of behaviour, e.g. 'behaves in a cheerful manner'. The statements also described Big Five characteristics. The categorizers were carefully trained and on average six of them judged each tape.

Each of the participants was also asked for the names of two people who knew them well and they in turn were asked first to describe the participant's personality, choosing from the set of 62 Big Five statements, and then to watch a tape of someone they didn't know and use the same set of statements to describe the personality of this person. Finally, a separate group rated the sets of statements on how likely they were to be valid cues in the particular setting (i.e. a five-minute filmed conversation between strangers). Here the researchers were studying beliefs or 'implicit personality theories'. In summary, the researchers had three sets of data for each participant:

1. their behaviour in two brief one-to-one conversations with different strangers;
2. a description of their personality, in terms of five factor theory, by people who knew them well;
3. judgements of their personality, in terms of five factor theory, by categorizers who did not know them.

For clarity I will leave out the results on implicit personality theories and give only the cues with correlations of 0.25 and above. This is partly for simplicity and for practical use and partly because the data, though of good quality, are less substantial than Thorne and Gough's (1991). Taking extraversion (EI in MBTI terms) first, the most valid cues, in the sense that observations from the tape and observations by people who know the person well in everyday life agreed with each other, are shown in Table 6.2.

Table 6.2: Valid cues for E and I (adapted from Funder and Sneed, 1993)

E	Is expressive in face, voice or gestures
	Has high enthusiasm
	Speaks in a loud voice
	Exhibits social skills
	Is talkative
I	Expresses insecurity or sensitivity
	Has awkward interpersonal style
	Behaves in a fearful or timid manner
	Is reserved and unexpressive
	Keeps partner at a distance
	Shows lack of interest in interaction

Extraversion and introversion are among the most visible personality characteristics. A bias against I may also be apparent. Clues for TF are in Table 6.3.
Like the standard five factor descriptions, the terms for TF in Table 6.3 are less
glowing than those on the Report Form for the MBTI. They are, however,
consistent with them and, by definition, observable and valid cues for T and F.
Surprisingly, SN and JP were less visible and the cues seemed to overlap with
those for the other factors. However, other research (e.g. Thorne and Gough,
1991) has found useful cues for both (see Chapter 2).

Tables 6.3: Valid cues for T and F (adapted from
Funder and Sneed, 1993)

T	'Acts irritable'
	Talks at, not with, partner
	Expresses scepticism or cynicism
F	Behaves in a cheerful manner
	Laughs frequently

Popular but possibly invalid cues

Turning to the cues actually used by observers (and with a relationship of 0.30
or above), these largely agreed with the valid cues. Those listed in Table 6.2
were used to judge E and I, plus 'initiates humour' and 'dominates the interaction'. 'Expresses interest in fantasy and daydreams' was used to identify N;
those listed in Table 6.3 were used for T and F, plus 'interrupts partner' for T;
'displays ambition', 'shows genuine interest in intellectual matters', 'exhibits
high degree of intelligence' were the cues (valid or not!) used for J; and there
were no cues at 0.30 or above for P.

Overall, Funder and Sneed's (1993) data support the view that people tend to
use the cues they think they use and use valid cues the most when judging
Extraversion (EI) and Agreeableness (TF). The study also supports the validity
of these two characteristics and the consistency of personality (because the
behaviours observed in the filmed conversations correlated with judgements by
people who knew those filmed in everyday life).

Funder and Sneed noted limitations of their study. For example, the 62
behaviours rated were a broad but far from exhaustive sample and perhaps they
did not include the most relevant behavioural cues, particularly for Openness
(SN). A particularly interesting suggestion is that accurate judgements may be
based on the careful weighting of numerous low validity cues rather than a few
highly valid ones. A more extreme version of this view was put forward in
another recent study. Here, accuracy was strongly linked to **overall** impressions; although these are vaguer and fuzzier, they were found to be generally

more useful than specific behaviours (Ambady and Rosenthal, 1993, p. 439). Ambady and Rosenthal give the example of a smile, which can be interpreted as positive, e.g. genuinely warm, or negative, e.g. threatening, depending on accompanying behaviour and context. Nevertheless, the cues identified by Funder and Sneed still (a) provide some validity evidence for E, I, T and F particularly, (b) may refine their meaning a little, and (c) may help observers, even those making more general judgements like 'warm', to be accurate more often.

Speculative cues

In the effort after meaning, we can see meaning where none exists, e.g. in tea leaves, shadows and stars. A similar phenomenon is noticing a broad relationship, e.g between neat clothing and a preference for J, and taking it too far, e.g. that clothes of a certain colour or style indicate a preference. Some such relationships may be true as tendencies; the error lies in the assumption that **all** cues are meaningful. Herrick (1987) offered many illustrations which could easily be tested formally: that Is tend to choose a softer look, EFs a small patterned design and ETs bolder, larger designs, Ns intricate patterns, Fs horizontal stripes and colours that blend, Ts vertical or diagonal stripes, and so on. She added that she had not found any relationships between colours and type.

Similarly, gestures may or may not be related to type. Scanlon (1988) reviewed Keirsey's suggestions for the four temperaments: that SPs point while they speak; SJs gesture very little but 'anchor' their hands in pockets, behind their backs, etc.; NTs 'draw' diagrams with their hands or number their points on their fingers; and that NFs gesture with open hands in flowing movements. Some or all of these ideas could be magical thinking supported by biased observation and memory, but they seem worth testing even though topic, setting and socialization are all likely to be influential. Handwriting seems to be unrelated to type (Bayne and O'Neill, 1988; Dean, 1992) but there appears to be a 'kernel of truth' in the idea that personality is revealed (to some extent) in the face (Berry and Finch Wero, 1993).

Questions to ask

Finally, good clues can be provided by answers to questions, both in their style and content. The EI preference is indicated by where the person's interest 'goes' most easily – outwards or inwards, in action or reflection – and by how they refresh themselves (see Chapter 2). There are some simple but not magical tests, e.g. ask an unexpected and novel question (novel to the person being asked). In theory, Es will tend to answer at once, Is to pause and reflect.

Choice of films and books (and style of and motives for reading) can be useful clues to SN, e.g. Ss tend to prefer more realistic books and to remember plots and details. For TF, the most obvious strategy is to ask the person to give their reasons for a decision or to analyse a problem or decision. Ts tend to present more reasons (which may include feelings) and in a logical, concise and easy way, Fs to say something 'felt right' or 'I just do'.

The JP preference should be relatively visible because it influences how we deal with the 'outside world'. Does the person organize easily, like to get on with things and get them done (J)? Like to keep gathering information (P)? Become quickly bored with routine (P)? Behave in an easygoing way (most of the time) (P)?

CONCLUSIONS

Accurate observation of people's preferences, temperaments and types is necessary for many applications of type theory. Despite a formidable number and variety of biases and obstacles, a reasonable level of accuracy is achieved in everyday life and can probably be improved on. Among the strategies are knowing the biases and trying to allow for them, looking for evidence against an observation as well as for it, knowing what evidence to look for and looking for alternative interpretations of that evidence.

Type and counselling

7

Four ways in which type theory and the MBTI can be applied to counselling are discussed in this chapter. They are that type can:

1. help counsellors understand, empathize with and accept clients whose personalities are very different from their own. This potential for quicker and deeper understanding and rapport is particularly important in brief counselling. Type can also encourage recognition and use of clients' strengths, easily overlooked when concentrating on problems, and, similarly, be useful as a framework for giving feedback to counsellors on their counselling;
2. suggest which forms of counselling and which strategies are most likely to be effective with clients of a particular type and those which are less likely. The problem of wanting to lose weight is used to illustrate this application;
3. explain, in part, counsellors' choice of theoretical orientation;
4. be a useful perspective on change in clients and on how effective counselling is likely to be with which characteristics and problems.

In this chapter I will discuss each aspect in turn, focusing particularly on how it can be used in counselling (the 'Once I know a client's dominant function, what do I do with it?' question). I'd also like to make three preliminary points, the first two to do with how I define counselling and the third with the use I make of research and ideas from five factor theory (discussed in Chapter 2).

I take an integrative approach to counselling, of the kind illustrated in Table 7.1. By 'integrative', I mean that this model allows the counsellor to use a variety of approaches within it, but in a systematic way. Person-centred ideas dominate Stage One in which the goals are to develop a working alliance and to help clients explore. Counsellors are empathic, accepting and genuine. In Stage Two, the goal is for clients to see their problems differently: counsellors continue to be empathic, accepting and genuine but add challenging skills. Cognitive counselling is an example of a possibly relevant approach here. Stage Three is concerned with action and ending. Several authors discuss variations of this model of counselling theory and practice (for example, Dryden and Feltham, 1992; Brammer *et al.*, 1993; Bayne *et al.*, 1994). The model fits well with type theory: different preferences are the most relevant to each stage, most notably I, S, F and P (Stage One), N and T (Two), and E and J (Three).

Table 7.1: A three-stage model of counselling

Stage One: Support
The counsellor accepts and empathizes with the client and is genuine. The client explores their reaction to a problem.

Stage Two (if necessary): Challenge or new perspectives
The counsellor suggests, or helps the client suggest, a new way of looking at the problem, then helps the client explore their reaction.

Stage Three (if necessary): Set goals and agree action
The counsellor helps the client decide what to do and how.

Second, my experience of counselling is with people who are suitable for relatively brief contracts, of three to 20 sessions, and who are not seriously disturbed. Therefore I will not discuss applications of type or the Big Five to conditions like severe depression and schizophrenia (see, for example, Widiger and Trull, 1992; Costa and Widiger, 1994). And third, I will draw on the Big Five literature, selecting those ideas and findings which seem particularly promising or useful from the perspective of the MBTI. Costa and McCrae (1992), McCrae (1991), McCrae and Costa (1991) and Miller (1991) are the main sources.

Miller (1991) comments that psychotherapy is 'difficult to practise and impossible to master', because people are 'astoundingly diverse' (p. 416). He captures key aspects of that diversity in the following paragraph, which (apart from the first aspect, which refers to neuroticism) correspond to the four pairs of preferences, in the order EI, NS, FT and JP:

Some clients suffer excessively from life's inevitable bumps and jolts, whereas others seem to endure them without apparent difficulty, seeking help only in reaction to severe stressors. Some clients arrive for the therapy hour saying, 'Thank God I'm here! I need so badly to talk. I didn't think I could make it through the week', but others consistently dread the therapy hour and feel relieved when it is over. Some clients are intrigued by an invitation to engage in a conversation with the ghost of their dead grandmother in an empty chair, whereas others find it exquisitely uncomfortable to behave in such a peculiar manner. Some clients are eager to accept the putative wisdom and good intentions of the therapist, but others assume the therapist is a fraud or a fool until they see evidence to the contrary. Some clients will assiduously work toward goals established in the therapy hour, willing to endure discomfort and fatigue in exchange for the promise of personal growth, whereas others 'forget' about behavioural goals and homework assignments, holding back from change if changing requires effort or pain. (pp. 416–17)

EMPATHY

Empathy can be defined as entering into someone's inner world and communicating to them your sense of it. It has an 'aroused, active, reaching out nature' (Barrett-Lennard, 1993) and usually seeks to capture both the content of the client's words and at least some of the emotion experienced by the client.

Type theory illustrates in a very concrete way how difficult empathy can be, offers an explanation of why it is difficult and suggests some constructive actions to develop and communicate it more quickly. At the most general level, it can be very helpful to know that there are people who are the opposite of yourself in some respects and that is not perverse or weird of them. More specifically, some of the individual differences in clients' behaviour and experience in counselling highlighted by type theory are listed in Table 7.2. Making a provisional judgement of a client's type or temperament will in itself help you to be less influenced by first impressions and more open to understanding the client as an individual (Chapter 6 discussed strategies for observing type more accurately.)

Table 7.2 draws directly on type theory at the level of four pairs of personality characteristics (Chapter 2). It is therefore not a speculative list; these characteristics are firmly based in the validity research on type and on the Big Five reviewed in Chapter 2. People tend to behave in these ways. In the initial counselling session or the early part of it, politeness, expectations of the client role and other factors may mean the client behaves uncharacteristically, but this will probably not be sustained. The ideas in earlier chapters about type development, type falsification and type dynamics will all be relevant to some clients.

The Big Five literature is consistent with Table 7.2 though, not surprisingly, more evaluative and less positive in tone. Miller (1991) suggests, for example, that clients low on Agreeableness (i.e. who prefer thinking) are more likely to be sceptical of the value of counselling, or of you as a counsellor, and may also not be interested in counselling because of a lack of interest in how they affect others. Type theory would express this characteristic as undeveloped feeling, with scope for its development. Similarly, clients who are low on Conscientiousness (who prefer perceiving) are seen as less likely to work in a systematic and disciplined way on managing a problem. Type theory would qualify this both in terms of development of the judging preference and for introverted perceiving types, because their dominant function is either thinking or feeling.

The implications of Table 7.2 for how the counsellor might behave most effectively with each client follow fairly directly. For example, if you are an extravert counsellor with an introvert client you might deliberately talk less than

Table 7.2: The preferences and clients' probable behaviour during counselling (developed from Bayne *et al.*, 1994, Miller, 1991, and Myers and McCaulley, 1985)

Clients who prefer:	tend to:
Extraversion	want a more active counsellor be less comfortable with reflection be optimistic and energetic
Introversion	be more at ease with silence be less comfortable with action be less enthusiastic about counselling
Sensing	be concrete and detailed go step by step like a 'practical' approach not see many options be uncomfortable with novelty
Intuition	give broad pictures jump around from topic to topic see unrealistic options see lots of options overlook facts like novelty and imaginative approaches
Thinking	avoid emotions, feelings and values in early sessions need rationales and logic be critical and sceptical want to be admired be competitive
Feeling	focus on values and networks of values need to care (e.g. about a value, a person or an ideal) be 'good clients' want to be appreciated
Judging	fear losing control find change stressful need structure need to achieve work hard and tolerate discomfort
Perceiving	avoid decisions need flexibility avoid discomfort

usual, or less than you would with an extravert client, or you might discuss the difference between you with your client. Similarly, the counsellor might be more concrete and pragmatic with clients who prefer sensing (but also be aware of their tendency to miss options); more experimental with intuitives (but perhaps also helping them to focus); aware of the tendency of clients with a feeling preference to like to please and therefore to be too good a client, and ready to challenge it gently, because feeling types also tend to be more sensitive to criticism; ready **not** to press thinking types on their emotions, especially early in counselling; more formal with judging types (but also ready to challenge them to plan some 'play'); and more informal with perceiving types (but also ready to challenge them to plan a little more).

Little is known empirically about the effect of personality characteristics on counselling as a process or on outcome (Garfield, 1986), though one of the preferences – introversion (though not measured by the MBTI) – has been studied in counselling itself. Nocita and Stiles (1986) contrasted two views of introverts as clients in counselling sessions: either they would tend to find it uncomfortable or counselling's inward focus might be congenial. They studied the average impact of sessions on 83 adult clients, mostly aged between 18 and 23, whose problems included depression, anxiety, low self-esteem, etc. The 24 counsellors were clinical psychology graduates in their second to fourth year of training and with a wide range of theoretical orientations.

The main finding was that on average introverts rated their sessions as 'relatively uncomfortable, unpleasant, tense, rough and difficult' and their mood after sessions as 'relatively unfriendly, uncertain, sad, angry and afraid' (Nocita and Stiles, 1986, p. 235). The effect was a substantial one. Nocita and Stiles recognize that distress is not necessarily a bad thing, but also that it can lead to premature ending or less effective counselling. Accordingly, counsellors could be particularly aware of the greater chance of discomfort in introverts, look for cues and consider compensating or allowing for it. With extraverts, especially EJs, there is a different kind of problem related to distress: they can seem so confident that signs of discomfort can easily be missed.

Provost (1984) recommends that counsellors first 'talk the language' of each client's type and then gradually 'pull back somewhat to their own style' (p. 129). I suspect this asks most counsellors to be too versatile and at worst will seem false. Moreover, being open and accepting (i.e. non-judgemental) about a difference between counsellor and client is more achievable and less tiring than switching preferences back and forth, and models good communication. On the other hand, some adaptation to the other person's 'language' happens routinely in conversations and is part of empathy.

Considerable flexibility on the part of the counsellor may be very desirable at certain points in counselling, for example when negotiating a contract or when the client is setting goals. Thus, ENTP or ENFP counsellors might encourage ISTJ and ISFJ clients to take action steps which are too large and need to be ready to give them 'space' to reflect and to say 'I'd like to think about that'.

The most difficult clients, according to type dynamics, are likely to be those whose dominant function is the counsellor's fourth function. Counsellors with dominant sensing, therefore, are predicted to find the strengths related to intuition in Table 7.2 the most difficult, and so on. Table 9.5 (p. 142) lists the most likely sources of conflict. A complexity here is that, especially for short periods, the opposite type can be unusually attractive as they are developed in ways we would like to be. Moreover, similarity can cause problems too, though of a different kind to oppositeness. Two Fs, for example, can have opposed values. More likely is that in all pairs and most groups, some dominant and auxiliary functions will be missing and therefore the activities associated with them will either be done with more effort or neglected. Table 7.2 indicates the likely effects on counselling if the latter occurs. For example, P counsellors with P clients will tend to find goal-setting and endings less salient.

I would like to emphasize two aspects of type and counselling as a process. First, a word for clients who prefer thinking and whom the counsellor sees as defensive because they avoid emotions. They may be defensive but they may also be behaving like developed thinking types and will focus on emotions in time. As is often the case in counselling, it is a question of going at the right pace, at any one moment choosing to be supportive or challenging and hoping to make the right choice most of the time. Second, all types can be effective counsellors and clients in their different ways. Provost (1984) provides excellent illustrations of this principle for clients. Her book contains brief 'case' studies of her counselling with a client of each type plus an INP and a 'room-mate conflict'.

The counsellor may choose to share type theory or parts of it with a client. Whether to do so and when are matters of clinical judgement and sensitivity. Rarely, for example, would a counsellor suggest completing the MBTI in crisis counselling or before sufficient trust had developed. On the other hand, an idea from type theory, e.g. about kinds of people, could be offered at many points. Guidelines on how to introduce the MBTI and interpret the results are at the beginning of Chapter 2.

The likely strengths and 'aspects to work on' of counsellors of different types are listed in Table 7.3. This kind of framework can be used in counsellor training to give feedback. It is also a useful counter to myths about 'the good counsellor'. The most effective way to use it (other strategies may work best for different types or stage of type development) may be to develop and confirm the skills and qualities associated with your dominant function first, then your auxiliary and so on. Thus strengths are built on and 'aspects to work on' are seen as the 'other side' of those strengths. The idea here is that the effect will be a less defensive, more constructive attitude towards the aspects to work on.

The counselling terms used in Table 7.3, e.g. paraphrasing, empathy, challenging, are in quite general use, though with some variations of meaning (Bayne et al., 1994). More paraphrasing is suggested for both extraverts and introverts but for different reasons: Es because they tend to emphasize self-expression more than listening, Is because they tend to listen in a passive way rather than actively checking.

Table 7.3: The preferences and aspects of counselling (from Bayne, 1993)

	Likely strengths	Likely skills to use more and aspects to work on
E	Helping the client explore a wide range of issues. Easy initial contact Thinking 'on feet'	Paraphrasing more Using silence Helping client explore issues in sufficient depth Reaching the action stage too early
I	Helping the client explore a few issues in depth. Reflecting on strategies, etc. Using silence	Paraphrasing more Helping the client move to action Helping client explore all relevant issues Ease of initial contact
S	Observing details Being realistic Helping client decide on practical action plans	Taking the overall picture into account Brainstorming (strategies, challenges and actions) Using hunches
N	Seeing the overall picture Brainstorming Using hunches	Being specific Testing hunches Helping client decide on practical action plans
T	Being objective Challenging (i.e. from counsellor's frame of reference)	'Picking up' feelings Being empathic (i.e. in client's frame of reference) Being warmer Challenging too early
F	Being warm Being empathic	Taking thoughts into account as well as feelings Coping with conflict and 'negative' emotions Being more objective Challenging
J	Being organized Being decisive	Helping client to make decisions (but not prematurely) Being flexible
P	Being spontaneous Being flexible	Being organized, e.g. keeping to time, structure of session Helping client to make decisions

MATCHING CLIENTS AND METHODS

There are several interesting suggestions in discussions of five factor theory and counselling about matching clients and methods, translated in this section into type terms. I will include those ideas that seem to fit type theory best, also drawing on discussions of type and counselling, e.g. Provost (1984). Most of the ideas are speculative at the moment.

Three cautions are particularly relevant. First, clients' personalities include all the preferences (as well as other qualities) and their behaviour will often be influenced by more than one characteristic at a time. The second caution is the obvious strategy for responding to this problem: to treat the suggestions as guidelines only, to be checked and negotiated. Third, counsellors, too, vary in which methods they are more or less comfortable with and in the range of methods they are prepared to work with (or, in some cases, can or should work with). Type theory, here as elsewhere, respects these differences.

The two pairs of preferences most relevant to choice of method are EI and SN. Client-centred and group counselling is suggested for extraverts and cognitive and Gestalt counselling for introverts, on the basis that extraverts tend to be more sociable and talkative while introverts find spontaneous speech more difficult. Clients who prefer sensing tend to be less comfortable with fantasy and more down to earth and may therefore be seen as 'resistant'. Conversely, clients who prefer intuition may be seen by counsellors (who tend to be intuitive types themselves) as more interesting: they are likely to be more unconventional, more open to novelty and fantasy. Counselling methods vary in the same way: cognitive–behavioural methods are practical and full of common sense in a way that guided fantasies and dream interpretation are not. Generally, it is easy to rank methods on an SN dimension and to predict that, in general, clients will respond best to the methods which resemble this part of themselves.

Of course, some clients benefit from methods they dislike; the value of using type then is that it provides a rationale for the counsellor's suggestion and for any difficulties that may arise.

I'd like to discuss type theory as applied to an area which many clients and others are upset, worried and frustrated about: trying to lose weight through dieting. Trying to create a perfect or at least a better body is part of Western culture and usually it involves being slim and physically fit (Brownell, 1991). At one level, this is generally straightforward: it is a matter of eating less, and healthily, and exercising more. At another level, it is very complicated. For example, many ways of trying to lose weight are counterproductive; people can feel like frauds because of the amount of time and energy they spend on looking good and both dieting and exercise can become obsessive (Ogden, 1992, c.f. Brownell and Rodin, 1994).

It now seems clear that most people have a fairly stable 'set point' for their weight and that we vary in the weight and body shape that is healthy for us, in the same way as we vary in eye colour. Part of responding to clients who want to lose weight is therefore (in Stage Two) to challenge their view of their appearance and its significance and the emotional and physical energy they're taking up. Ogden (1992), for example, argues that being thinner does **not** make people happier and that there are benefits to **not** dieting: greater self-acceptance, more energy, avoiding failure in this respect (most diets fail) and health ('yo-yo' dieting may be unhealthy). Paradoxically, the person may then lose weight more readily and not put it back on.

Given all the above, type theory suggests some strategies for clients who feel despairing. Counsellors too can feel despairing about clients who fail to lose weight. For example, Miller (1991) writes, as one of several vivid examples of a mismatch between effort and desire in clients low in Conscientiousness:

> A woman who has hated herself for years because she is overweight is encouraged to keep an eating diary and calculate her daily calorie intake. Despite continuing encouragement, she never buys a calorie counter and never records any of her meals. Her explanation is she is afraid she will be upset if she learns how much she really eats. We agree that it might be a good thing if she got upset about her eating habits. She continues to claim that low self-esteem due to obesity is her main problem, and she never complies with the plan. (p. 430)

Miller sees this client as a particular kind of person, not as resistant, and he is inclined to see her as unable to change. But type offers a strategy, or rather a set of strategies, which he didn't try. People with a marked preference for perceiving tend to resent rules and plans to control eating. Rather, they find it easier to go on what Scanlon (1986) calls a 'sort of' diet, 'eating the same foods but less of them' (p. 2). The same principle applies to Ps and exercise: a little more or a little more often, but not plans, schedules and routines.

Scanlon suggests strategies for each of the four temperaments and 16 types, based on theory and illustrated with anecdotes. Table 7.4 is a summary of her ideas on temperament and clients. It is speculative and incomplete. The main point, though, is that different strategies seem most likely to work for each of the types – or at least are worth discussing with a client from that point of view.

Scanlon further suggests that SPs are less likely to need to diet, because they are more 'in touch with' hunger and fullness (like the infants discussed in Chapter 1). To develop, or rediscover, this introverted sensing ability, ask 'Am I hungry?', 'What exactly do I want to eat?' and, at intervals, 'Am I full yet?'. The types least likely to have developed sensing are the dominant intuitives: INJs and ENPs.

In contrast, SJs are expected to respond well to conventional methods of losing weight – lots of goals which can be worked towards systematically and steadily – especially if they see it as an issue of responsibility. Kroeger (1985) adds (for SJs): 'Look at your food, smell it, identify the different flavours'. And 'find an authority figure to report to' (p. 17). As a further contrast, NTs tend to be motivated best by competition and to need an overview of medical knowledge, etc. Kroeger also suggests that they design their own diet.

Table 7.4: The temperaments and approaches to effective dieting (summarized from Scanlon, 1986)

SP	Prefer to eat when hungry or on impulse Don't like to plan Want fun Focus on process more than goals
SJ	Like planned mealtimes Can be very task-focused, strong-willed and organized
NT	Need a clear rationale and overview Like to be in control of their body and efficient Less likely to be 'in touch' with their body (because of their more abstract, impersonal nature)
NF	Need to find a personal meaning in dieting (food as symbol) Try to cooperate with their body rather than control it Will diet when it feels right Likely to diet in bursts (lots of different diets) May need to diet for someone else (for love)

See Table 3.5 on motives associated with dominant functions and Table 3.7 on motives and temperament

For NFs, Kroeger (1985) suggests that unhappiness about weight is usually about something else (which needs to be worked out) and also that they are the least likely group to have a realistic picture of themselves and the most likely to feel guilty. Guilt, of course, can lead to overeating. Kroeger's main suggestion for NFs, therefore, is to work on themselves, leaving the actual diet for later.

However, some of the speculations outlined above imply type differences in being overweight and King *et al.* (1993), in a study of 2633 male and female students, did not find such differences. Nor did Harris (unpublished, cited in King *et al.* (1993)) who studied five groups: people who had never had weight problems; people who had successfully lost weight without outside help; people who had successfully lost weight with outside help; people who had tried to lose weight but failed; and people who were overweight and had not attempted to lose weight.

Two limitations of the King *et al.* study are that nearly all their participants were aged between 18 and 21 and they reported their own heights and weights. The problem with age is that type theory (as noted above) suggests that **developed** ISs, for example, should be overweight less often than other types. The authors note that the evidence on the accuracy of self-report data on weight is mixed. However, 19% of their participants were classified as overweight, so there was an opportunity for relationships with type to be found – and none were. King *et al.* conclude (1) that further research on type and being overweight seems unpromising but (2) that type might still be useful in choosing strategies for losing weight.

Type provides a similar perspective on making love. Some suggestions from Scanlon (1992) are outlined in Table 7.5. As with much of type theory, they are matters of emphasis.

Table 7.5: The preferences and making love (summarized from Scanlon, 1992)

E	Talk and be direct
I	Don't talk
S	'Stay present, stay physical'
N	Talk about broader, personal things
T	Work on improving your skills
F	Romance first. Need to be 'in the mood' more
J	Give notice or have a routine
P	Surprise. Unusual times and places

c.f. Table 9.5

Type then (1) implies a general strategy for managing problems – raising awareness that there are strategies other than the standard ones and that the standard ones are not suitable for all types, and (2) may also be helpful in matching each strategy/method with each type or temperament. However, both implications need to be seen within the general perspective on change which type and five factor theory share.

CHANGE

The effectiveness of counselling is now firmly established (Lambert *et al.*, 1986; Barkham, 1993). Three contrasting views about its degree of effectiveness are:

1. that there is an enormous capacity for change;
2. that only modest change is likely;
3. that the degree of change seems modest but is actually very worthwhile.

On the first view, personality change happens frequently through life events like divorce, midlife crises or finding a better job. Indeed, self-help books often claim that reading them is enough to bring about significant change.

Taking the second view, Smail (1987) saw counselling as 'much less help than almost any of us can bear to think'. He also saw this as desirable: people are not changed as if, in Anthony Clare's term, counselling is a 'psychic launderette'. Life would be trivial if we were: 'People *grow* from one position to the next, they cannot be *switched*' (Smail, 1987, p. 89). Similarly, Zilbergeld (1983) argues that we tend to hear about the dramatic 'cures' when often it is more a matter of, for example, reducing the number of episodes of depression per year and their intensity rather than someone being transformed. A problem here for counsellors is that many believe that people are always capable of personal growth and Zilbergeld's cautious position sounds pessimistic.

Both type theory and five factor theory share the view that people are limited in their capacity for change (e.g. McCrae, 1993), but they are not pessimistic about it. They suggest that modest expectations are both appropriate and of great value, because the degree of effectiveness only appears to be modest. For example, Rosenthal (1990) compared counselling's effects with medical research on aspirin and heart attacks. The effectiveness of aspirin is about 4%, i.e. if 100 people who have had a heart attack take aspirin, four more of them on average will avoid another heart attack compared with 100 people who have had a heart attack but do not take aspirin. This degree of effectiveness was acclaimed as a major breakthrough. Counselling's average effect size is 10%. Several studies in organizations have shown greater effects, e.g. the UK Post Office found a 50% reduction in absence from work after an average of three counselling sessions (Allinson *et al.*, 1989).

The starting position of five factor theory and type is that the major personality characteristics are fairly consistent throughout life, but that what can change more is a person's attitude towards themselves, their habits and roles. This is not to say that we know what the limits of change are, let alone what they will be with new methods, but that on current evidence, for major genetically-based personality characteristics, there are clear limits. Moreover, it suggests a circumstance when change should be relatively **easy**: when a client has developed a false type but has decided to express their true type more. However, then of course they are not changing at the level of genetic predisposition.

A more analytical approach is needed: which characteristics of people are relatively stable and therefore by definition hard or impossible to change, and which are more open to change? Happiness is an example of a stable characteristic, embodied in the idea that some people are generally cheerful by disposition and others more gloomy. And Costa *et al.* (1987) show that happiness over a ten-year span can be predicted 'far more accurately' from measures of past happiness than from factors like gender, age or transitions, i.e. most people adapt quite quickly to events like divorce, bereavement and unemployment.

Similarly, major personality characteristics as summarized by the Big Five are stable in adulthood, over periods of up to 30 years (Costa and McCrae, 1986, 1994). Costa and McCrae emphasize the radical changes in most people's circumstances during 30 years and yet basic personality characteristics change little: 'People surely grow and change, but they do so on the foundation of enduring dispositions' (1994, p. 36). Like Rosenthal, however, they do not see this as a reason for gloom. They argue that it should lead to more realistic expectations. Attempts to change personality are not likely to succeed, but some

behaviour does change and so do attitudes. And they too compare counselling with drug treatment: 'The effect may be so small that thousands of subjects must be tested to produce significant results. Yet the findings are quite properly hailed as a breakthrough, because the few percentage point gains are multiplied by the hundreds of thousands of victims of the disease, the millions of hours of work lost, the billions spent on medical treatment' (1986, p. 420).

Moreover, some characteristics which people want to change are more malleable. Assertiveness training, for example, is effective for a wide range of problems and skills, depression and panic attacks can now be treated quite quickly and economically, study skills can be learned and so on. But distinctions are needed between developmental change, deliberate attempts to change basic personality and deliberate attempts to change maladaptive behaviours.

Miller's (1991) clinical experience is in agreement with the finding that basic personality is stable. For example, his view of clients markedly low in Conscientiousness (C) (i.e. who prefer perceiving and have undeveloped judging) is:

> I have tried interpretation, confrontation, treatment contracts, paradoxical approaches, self-monitoring, and other methods with little apparent success. Low C might represent one of the absolute limits to the power of psychotherapy. It may be that for very low C clients treatment must be primarily palliative or supportive. (pp. 430–1).

Type theory, not surprisingly, is more evenhanded: clients high in judging may be too disciplined and conscientious, just as those high on feeling may be 'too nice', too cooperative. Type theory, to a greater extent than Miller (1991), sees potential problems associated with both high and low Conscientiousness (both J and P). It is also rather more optimistic about people's capacity for development of the 'other side' of themselves.

COUNSELLOR ORIENTATION

Type theory suggests that each counsellor is likely to be most comfortable and effective with a particular approach, stage and associated skills of counselling, depending on their psychological type (see Table 7.3). For example, counsellors who prefer sensing will tend to be more skilled at observing non-verbal cues than at detecting themes and patterns. Two studies of general orientation and type have been reported: McBride and Martin (1988) and Erickson (1993).

McBride and Martin (1988) asked 64 graduate counselling students on a Master's course to identify their 'primary counselling theory'. They distinguished between two broad possibilities: affective (client-centred, Gestalt and existential) and cognitive (RET, Adlerian, reality and behavioural). Two immediately obvious limitations of the study, therefore, are the relative lack of experience of the participants and the very basic classification of approaches to counselling.

Their main findings were as follows: of the 21 counsellors who preferred thinking, 17 chose cognitive approaches and four chose affective approaches, and of the 43 counsellors who preferred feeling, 24 chose affective approaches and 19 chose cognitive. Thus, Ts clearly preferred cognitive approaches while Fs chose both more equally. Looking at the types, much the most frequent were the ENFPs. Fourteen ENFPs chose affective and seven, cognitive. More striking, there were four ISTJs, two INTJs, two ESTJs and five ENTJs (these are the four TJ types) and all but one of these chose cognitive, consistent with a task-oriented, analytical approach.

On the other hand, dominant function did not prove a more powerful factor than auxiliary in choice of counselling orientation. For example, three of the four INFPs chose cognitive and so did the only two ESFJs and two of the five ENFJs. For the ESFJs, the more practical emphasis of cognitive approaches could explain their choice (an explanation more consistent with temperament theory than type), but this would not be the case for the INFPs and ENFJs.

Analysis of McBride and Martin's data in terms of temperament gives the following:

	SP	SJ	NT	NF
Cognitive	2	8	12	14
Affective	2	6	2	18

Overall, thinking was the most influential factor, especially combined with Intuition.

Erickson (1993) asked 23 counsellors aged from 30 to 55 to rank order seven major approaches to counselling and, like McBride and Martin, categorized them into cognitive and affective approaches.

She analysed her data in three ways and found the same general pattern in each. The methodological replication of Martin and McBride produced the following: five of the seven counsellors who preferred thinking chose a cognitive approach and 12 of 16 F counsellors chose an affective approach, particularly client-centred. Erickson points out that this pattern – that counsellors tend to choose counselling theories which are consistent with their types – has practical implications. She suggests that counsellors need to be aware of the limiting effect of this in choosing what might be the most effective strategy for clients. I'd add that one general strategy is to consider referring clients to other counsellors more often (Bayne et al., 1994).

One other study of type and counselling is worth mentioning. Martin et al. (1985) found that 90% of a group of 37 counsellors working with blind clients preferred sensing, when counsellors in general tend to prefer intuition. The authors speculate that this is perhaps because sensing skills – the work was rehabilitation counselling – are best taught by sensing types, but also note that their work included a lot of administration.

The general research area of type and orientation is promising but needs more specific analysis of preferred models (and ideally of models actually used rather than espoused models). Choice of techniques would also be of interest, as would problems experienced as most and least difficult.

CONCLUSIONS

1. Type theory may help counsellors empathize more deeply and more quickly. It makes empathy a more tangible idea and also illustrates how difficult it is.
2. Clients and counsellors of different types tend to behave differently in counselling and to be more comfortable with different aspects of counselling.
3. For applications to particular problems, type suggests a straightforward basic principle: use a strategy which appeals to your client's dominant function or temperament or at least does not go directly against them.
4. Type theory could make referral more acceptable by reducing feelings of failure, rejection or inadequacy on the parts of both clients and counsellors.
5. Type suggests that change in basic personality is very unlikely. Paradoxically, this idea can be seen as optimistic.
6. Counsellors' preferred orientations appear to be related to type, particularly for thinking types.

8	# Type and education

The main theme of this chapter is that radically different ways to learn appear to be best for different people. Being told, in effect, that 'This is the (one) best way to study, etc.' is unhelpful for most people. At the least, type theory spells out a wide range of options and suggests why each of us tends to be biased towards some of these and against others. At best, it cuts down the guesswork about which options and strategies are most and least comfortable, and most and least effective, for which people.

I will focus on four aspects of type and education: styles of learning, styles of teaching, giving and receiving 'feedback', and writing. The main general sources on type and education are Lawrence (1993) and Murphy (1992, especially Chs 8–13).

LEARNING STYLES

Type respects our capacity to know when we have found ways of doing things which suit us and suggests guidelines for each type and temperament in order to make discovering them easier and quicker. The ideas are usually expressed as relationships between each preference and learning style rather than between type and learning style, but the dominant function should in theory be the most relevant preference. Thus an ESTJ is predicted to learn best using an ET style and an ISFP using an IF style.

Table 8.1 summarizes the main ideas on learning styles from Jensen (1987, especially Figure 1), Dutton (1992) and Lawrence (1993). The phrases indicate the kind of situation which seems likely to 'suit' each preference and dominant function. An extraverted thinking style needs action and analysis, for example. This is not to say that the ET types need continual action and analysis and nothing else! Rather, the argument is that each style (or situation which encourages that style) should be available for everyone, whatever their type. The problem, of course, is that generally only some of the styles are realistically available. The major factors in limiting the options seem likely to be simply tradition and the teacher's own type, as discussed in the section on teaching styles (p. 127).

Table 8.1: The preferences and learning styles (adapted from Lawrence, 1993)

Extraversion (E) Movement, action, talk, contact, discussion, group projects, trial-and-error	**Introversion (I)** Reflection Working individually
Sensing (S) Concrete to abstract, step by step, practical, specific directions	**Intuition (N)** Imaginative leaps, theory first, seeing relationships
Thinking (T) Logic and systems Analysis Challenge and sense of achievement	**Feeling (F)** Human aspects Feeling encouraged Studying topics they care about Harmonious atmosphere
Judging (J) Structure, goals, formality Prescribed tasks and completing them	**Perceiving (P)** Learning as 'a free-wheeling, flexible quest' (Jensen, 1987, p. 186) Choices Spontaneity Flexibility Work as play

Lawrence (1993, pp. 40–6) summarized the results of extensive research (over 130 studies) on learning styles. He sees the research as supporting type theory and therefore the styles summarized in Table 8.1. There are a few exceptions, e.g. action as a characteristic of Es' style has not been tested formally and would need to be defined specifically for this to happen. Teaching methods most compatible with each type are generally obvious. Lawrence lists methods associated with various combinations of preferences, as well as each preference on its own, and some vivid examples. Thus one student said 'I think better with my hands', took an alternator apart and at this point made sense of the diagram meant to guide him. He needed to use his sensing first, though, as Lawrence remarks, similar diagrams may be more useful to him in the future. In contrast, another student said of his mechanics class, 'All we do is stand around the cars and take parts off and put them back on'. He wanted books: symbols and principles. When they were available, though this was not until two weeks into the course by which time he might have left, he became more interested in understanding the machines.

Lawrence (1993) and Murphy (1992) suggest many ways of applying type to learning; a useful starting point is for the teacher to consider the effects of her or his own type and, therefore, most natural teaching style. Table 8.2 suggests another source of evidence and ideas on preferred learning styles and methods.

Table 8.2: Type and leisure (adapted from Provost, 1990)

ISTJ Tend to be serious and thorough. Computer games, Trivial Pursuit, golf, chess.	**ISFJ** Planned activities with close friends or relatives e.g. eating, Nature, TV.
ISTP Mechanical things. Shooting, scuba diving, stand-up comedy, tricks.	**ISFP** Quiet, friendly. Crafts, art.
ESTP Tend to be very active and competitive. Racing, boxing.	**ESFP** Tend to be very social, warm, friendly.
ESTJ Tend to organize and run things. Community organizations, and using their interest in Nature.	**ESFJ** Tend to be warm-hearted and enjoy planning parties and less competitive sports.
INFJ Tend to like reflective, solitary activities, e.g. music, reading, collecting.	**INTJ** Tend to be critical and serious. Games of strategy, museums, study.
INFP Private enthusiasms. Writing, photography, films, books, Nature.	**INTP** Tend to be solitary. Reading, chess.
ENFP Tend to be warmly enthusiastic about many kinds of leisure, e.g. reading fiction, acting.	**ENTP** Tend to need travel, adventure, unusual events.
ENFJ Tend to set up social events. Reading and the arts.	**ENTJ** Tend to organize groups, events that mix business and pleasure, competitive sports.

As a further illustration of ideas about type and learning style, consider the results of an exercise with groups of sensing and intuitive teachers who were asked to design a reading lesson to 'teach three vocabulary terms'. Murphy (1992) found that sensing teachers 'frequently' introduce each word, examine the letters, etc., define it, ask students to file each word into prewritten sentences, and finally to write new sentences. Intuitive teachers 'almost always' begin with a story which uses the three words several times (in her example, the words are 'exquisite', 'barrister' and 'maze'). They tend not to define the words. Sensing students said the intuitive activity sounded fun 'but wondered when the lesson would finally be taught ... that the story had so many words in it that by the end they weren't even sure which words they were expected to study' (Murphy, 1992, p. 80). Intuitive students loved the intuitive lesson and were bored by the sensing one.

Dutton (1992) changed the design of a training programme by offering a choice between a brief general case study and a detailed one and adapting exercises so that they could be done in pairs, threes or fours. It is also worth taking the extra step of showing a draft to a colleague with the opposite dominant function to your own. Their comments can be a revelation (see discussion of type and communication in Chapter 9, and the rest of this chapter).

TEACHING STYLES

Mismatches between teaching and learning styles are inevitable. Type theory suggests that teachers, tutors and lecturers should (a) continue predominantly with their own style, working from their strengths, and (b) add some recognition of the other styles. For example, intuitive lecturers could continue to concentrate on theories and concepts but include more facts, thinking teachers could praise as well as challenge, and so on. As Lawrence puts it, 'We can find teaching styles that accommodate the essential needs of our own types and at the same time provide a good learning environment for students of other types' (1993, p. 58). The alternative is a form of type falsification, producing what Jung called 'educational monstrosities' (Jensen, 1987, p. 188).

More specifically, the tutor can ask themselves: Have I provided for Es? For Is, etc.? Type concepts can be used fairly directly, e.g. 'Let's have some time to reflect quietly on this now' or 'That was a step by step account. What's an overview?'. With a group knowledgeable about type, type language itself can be used: 'Time for some introversion?'

Lawrence (1993) reviewed research on other aspects of teaching style. For example, consider the kinds of question you, or someone who tutors you, generally uses. Lawrence suggests that SN is the major influence. Intuitive teachers are more likely to ask overview questions: What are your impressions of ...? What's the main theme ...? What might happen if ...? Sensing teachers, in contrast, are more likely to ask for realism and detail: What did you see happening ...? What did she actually say ...? What was it about her manner ...? (Lawrence, 1993, pp. 76–7).

Tables 8.3 and 8.4 give two of the results of an interview study of teachers' perceptions and decisions about their teaching (by Thompson, described in Lawrence, 1993, pp 77–9). Other aspects of teaching style studied were the role of the teacher, where ideas for teaching come from, how teaching is planned, typical methods and when the teacher feels successful.

Table 8.3: Teacher type and planning (adapted from Lawrence, 1993)

ST	Detailed plans in advance for year and term, with specific objectives
SF	Detailed teaching plans taking students' abilities into consideration
NF	Plans structured around general goals, themes and students' needs; then adapting plan to students' needs week to week
NT	Plans follow an overall yearly structure, organized by concepts or themes

Table 8.4: Teacher type and evaluation (adapted from Lawrence, 1993)

ST	Use points and percentages in a systematic way
SF	Use points and percentages, plus extra credit options
NF	Use a number of factors, only one of which is grades
NT	Use a number of factors

Lawrence uses the findings in the following exercise:

1. Form four groups: ST, SF, NF, NT.
2. Respond to the aspects listed above.
3. Read the summaries from the study, e.g. those listed in Tables 8.3 and 8.4.
4. Discuss implications for modifying teaching style, i.e. using your strengths but adding some recognition for the strengths of the other psychological types.

Similarly, type influences exam questions. Murphy (1992) asked dominant function groups to design questions to assess understanding of a course on drugs. Sensing teachers focused on details of information, intuitive teachers on broad essay questions, thinking teachers on reasons and punishments, feeling teachers on how drugs affect people. Put so baldly, this sounds stereotypical but Murphy reports (though informally) that she has repeated this activity more than 20 times and that the results are consistent. A more formal account would be valuable but the practical implication would be the same: use a variety of questions to respect different strengths and preferences. Another factor would be the educational level of the exam.

Provost *et al.* (1987) studied the expression of their type's natural strengths by 'outstanding teachers of undergraduates'. Eighteen professors took part in the study, 14 men and four women from a variety of disciplines: English (7), religion/philosophy (3), anthropology/sociology (2), economics (2), biology (2), astronomy (1) and geography (1). The significance of the study lies not in any possible relationships between type and perceived excellence (obviously the judgements could be biased) but in relationships between type and how the professors wrote about their teaching at a time when, with one exception, they were unfamiliar with type theory.

The words and metaphors used by the different types are striking (though selected to illuminate type theory): 'the religious metaphors of the NFJs; the teacher as father from several ENTJs; images of "bonding" and mutuality from the NFPs and the "yardstick" and the "entrepreneur" terms of the STJs' (Provost *et al.*, 1987, p. 29). The professors also showed awareness of the limitations of their strengths as teachers and compensations for these. For example, an economics professor revealed his dominant thinking but also a place for his fourth function, feeling, when he wrote of his students:

> I want them to appreciate that they cannot solve problems unless they marshal facts, sift through data, and establish a framework for solving them. But I also want students to incorporate compassion and values into the solution of a problem. (p. 30)

GIVING AND RECEIVING FEEDBACK

One of the professors studied by Provost *et al.* (1987) commented that type theory 'casts a whole new light on reviewing student evaluations'. He was struck by the idea that positive and negative feedback about his teaching probably reflected different perceptions of his ENFP style by N students and S students. A related idea was illustrated in Table 7.3 on giving feedback, within a type framework, on counselling skills and qualities.

Strategies for making contact with students (and others) when commenting on their work follow directly from type theory. Tables 8.5 and 8.6 are summaries of Table 1 in Jensen and DiTiberio (1989). The impact of the feedback depends on type development, though; for example, an intuitive person who is actively developing her sensing will benefit from concrete examples more than when she is still putting most energy into intuition. In the same way, Jensen and DiTiberio recommend sometimes pairing students with the same preference but at different levels of development to comment on each other's work, and sometimes students of opposite preferences. Ideal feedback therefore depends to some extent on the person receiving it. I also wonder to what extent some of the ideas in Table 8.5 are true for people of all or most of the types, and how much good feedback is independent of type. As far as I know, no-one has studied this aspect of giving feedback. For those who mark essays or reports or write references, you may find a relationship between your own type and the sets of words in Table 8.6. You may also observe them as favourite concepts of certain colleagues!

Tables 8.5 and 8.6 are directly related to type theory and therefore valid to

Table 8.5: The preferences, giving feedback and making contact (adapted from Jensen and DiTiberio, 1989, Table 1)

E	I
Spoken feedback	Feedback in advance of discussion
S	**N**
Concrete examples	More conceptual and 'What if ...?' questions
T	**F**
Direct criticism and analysis	Personal contact and positive feedback first
About content	About style
J	**P**
Comments on organization and directed towards improving the next essay rather than this one	Comments on breadth and improving **this** essay

Table 8.6: The preferences and appealing 'words of praise' (adapted from Jensen and DiTiberio, 1989, Table 1)

E	I
Lively, vital, shows initiative	Thoughtful, shows depth
S	**N**
Realistic, careful, solid, practical	Imaginative, original
T	**F**
Analytic, logical, systematic	Interesting, enjoyable, personal, heartfelt
J	**P**
Complete, decisive, efficient	Questioning, open-minded, flexible

the extent that type theory is (Chapters 2 and 3). However, they still need investigating and refining, as in a study by Smith (1993). She investigated lecturers' preference for T or F and their marking style. TF is of particular significance because it contrasts two ways of evaluating. Smith compared the language used by six lecturers who preferred feeling and six who preferred thinking in their comments on the same essay. All 12 were INs and worked in an English department. Their ages ranged from 33 to 48 (with 10–25 years teaching experience) and four of the Fs and three of the Ts were women.

The lecturers all followed the same basic pattern of feedback: immediate comments in the margins and a summary at the end praising what was good, identifying one or two weaknesses and suggesting revisions. Both Ts and Fs wrote about the same amount, gave the same average mark and used similar numbers of questions, reactions, identifications (e.g. 'You have two ideas here') and directions (e.g. 'Look up the rules for commas').

The differences between the T and F groups were as follows. The lecturers who preferred feeling (five of whom were INFJs, therefore not dominant Fs) praised the essay twice as often as those who preferred T and wrote twice as many suggestions (e.g. 'You might try ...'). The actual figures, on the one essay assessed, were 6.5 praising remarks versus 3.5 and 5.3 suggestions versus 2.8. Smith comments that this implies different definitions of the student–teacher relationship and cites Jensen and DiTiberio's view that 'thinking types seem to value good content and organization over good style ... feeling types value the more personal qualities of writing' (1989, p. 137).

The particular essay marked in the study was written by a feeling student and characteristically it was not well organized and was argued emotionally rather than logically. The lecturers generally agreed on its main weakness and on a revision plan, yet the Ts and Fs differed in their style of comment and presumably in the impact of their feedback on the student. The survey element of Smith's research found that Fs reported greater concern about the possibility of hurting students' feelings while the Ts focused more on content and potential learning. It is as if Ts believe that the students' concern is the same as theirs: 'a concern with weaknesses and not strengths: what is the problem that needs solving?' (p. 40). Feeling students would tend not to share this belief and thinking students might not all be quite as positive about it as the lecturers. A particularly striking part of the research design (given the results) is that the English department works with agreed guidelines on assessment, which would be expected to reduce differences between the markers. On the other hand, a weakness is that the staff knew their MBTI results and that the guidelines included a deliberate attempt to balance T and F criteria.

This seems to me an exciting and fruitful new area for research. What can teachers of each of the types learn from each other about giving feedback? What are the effects of the other preferences on feedback? How do students of different types react to different styles of feedback?

WRITING

Writing is a mysterious activity. Both emotional and rational factors influence whether or not it happens and the style and quality of writing. I will take some of the factors involved, or thought to be involved, in writing, and then briefly discuss whether they seem generally applicable or more relevant to some psychological types than others. The factors are:

1. the effort most writers put into their writing;
2. a subtle reward from writing;
3. specific strategies.

Effort

Most writers rewrite several times. A few examples follow from, respectively, a novelist/professor of English, two professors of psychology and a professor of counselling. Malcolm Bradbury takes, say, four pages and writes instructions and comments on them as if he's marking an essay, rewrites and so on about ten times (Davies, 1978). Liam Hudson writes nine or ten drafts of 'absolutely everything' and comments that this is 'an immensely punishing process' (Cohen, 1976). Henri Tajfel is more specific about the results of all this effort: 'After five hours I have two pages covered ... you can do 20 pages in 50 hours so it's not too bad' (Cohen, 1976). Salomone (1993) recommends 'Be happy with two or three pages of written work (rough draft) per writing session' and 'Plan for seven to eight revisions (with one to two weeks between each)' (p. 76).

Knowing that successful writers work so hard (and the effort illustrated above seems quite typical) may help others change and demystify their concept of writing and either abandon writing or put in more effort themselves. To say 'I don't want to put that much effort in' or 'I don't have the stamina' is quite different from saying 'I just can't write'. Moreover, essays and reports require less polishing than articles and books.

Chance also plays a part. I remember finding one of my lecturers cutting sentences out of a manuscript (this was in the 1960s, long before word processors) and taping them into new positions, and being struck by how comfortable he was with this process. My assumption at that time, perhaps quite common – that writing either appeared in finished form or didn't, that you were either inspired or not – was very effectively challenged.

Reward

A subtle reward of writing is that it can clarify thinking. This idea – which can make writing seem more worth the effort – is that once you have written something down (brought it out into the open) then you can examine it more easily. It questions the opposite view that first you think clearly, then you write (Green and Wason, 1982). Writing is an act of discovery.

Specific strategies

Numerous strategies have been suggested to improve writing or even just to start writing:

- focus on or devise a title as early as possible;
- make a rough plan first (but do not necessarily stick to it);
- rewrite;
- ask friends and colleagues to comment on early drafts;
- set subgoals, e.g. write some of the references out, a draft of the introduction, or a table;

- pull an outline out **after** writing most of the first draft;
- incubate (patiently);
- read the material aloud;
- ask someone else to read it to you;
- find or devise a theme sentence for each paragraph;
- look out for unrealistic expectations about your writing;
- know that 'lows always follow highs' and so on (see, for example, Hayes and Flower, 1986; Boice, 1987; Hartley and Branthwaite, 1989; Sellers, 1991; Salomone, 1993).

Perhaps the most useful general strategy is suggested by Green and Wason (1982). They argue that writing something and writing it well require two different kinds of skill. Their strategy, therefore, is to separate the two processes. The first draft is written in as flowing and uncritical a state of mind as possible, which requires being open, trusting and tolerating apparent disorder. The second draft is evaluative, critical and concerned with grammar and style.

Psychological type and writing

I think there are two main questions about type and writing: are some of the various strategies more useful to some types than others, and is type recognizable from the finished writing? On the first question, Ching (1986), with a small group of 'mature writers' (17 academics), found that TJ writers tend to write only one draft with only minor changes to it and that NPs and Fs are most likely to revise a lot. Ching also found a 'scheduled, orderly, driving' quality in the Js.

The generalizations in Table 8.7 are derived from Jensen and DiTiberio (1989), a series of articles in *The Type Reporter* (Scanlon, 1990b), type theory and my own experience. These ideas and findings are obviously directly consistent with type theory and, most seductively, assume that there is a most natural way for each person to write. Extraverts, for example, may write best after talking about their ideas or by dictating them or by making writing seem more like speaking – the 'leaping in' idea – or pretending they are giving a talk. A second characteristic theme is to write from your strengths, especially your dominant function, first (mainly), and add more of the qualities associated with the strengths of other types later. (But if you're happy with your writing, leave it alone.) Third, there is another subtle theme here which recurs throughout type theory. Writers can be blocked by either trying to write in an unnatural way or by overdoing their natural way: Es keep talking rather than writing, Is reflecting and so on (Jensen and DiTiberio, 1989). And fourth, it can be very helpful to ask for feedback on your writing from people representing good development of each dominant function. But it's easy not to!

Finally, I'd like to say something about my own writing and to use an aspect of type theory to try to explain it. The distinction between dominant and

Table 8.7: The preferences and strategies to improve writing

E   Talk about the topic, then 'leap into writing'; perhaps outline later. *Add tough-minded rewriting and organizing.*

I   Plan first, in silence and alone: immerse yourself in the material and wait (*but not too long!*).

S   First drafts tend to be detailed. *Add the central ideas or themes and perhaps delete (let go) some of the detail.*

N   Ignore plans. *Add examples and detailed argument; delete (let go) some of the ideas.*

T   Focus on content rather than on the impact on the reader, write best following an outline or map, and in an objective style. *Add 'signposts' and more personal reactions later. Add more 'tact, flow and esthetics' (Scanlon).*

F   Write best about topics they care about. Find out how you feel about it first. Let the content flow. *Add evidence, analysis and opposing views.*

J   Focus and write their first drafts early. *Add any questions and doubts, however slight; some 'usuallys', 'seems', 'manys', and 'oftens'.*

P   Choose broad topics and revise extensively. *Add conclusions last (Js are more likely to start with them). Think of them as provisional but state them directly.*

How the preferences tend, in theory, to be related to aspects of writing, is in normal print. Suggested strategies are (a) to accept and if necessary develop those tendencies and (b) to add the strengths of some of the other preferences (in italics).

auxiliary functions is the important one. When I write, a struggle often takes place between my introverted feeling, my dominant function and a part of me which wants order and closure and values simplicity, and my extraverted intuition, my auxiliary which wants to include everything at all relevant and which is always looking for new ideas and new links. The resulting tension can be creative or futile. Ideally it is a partnership which, according to type theory, is at its best when the dominant function actually does dominate and the auxiliary function contributes to it.

In introverts, there is a risk of the extraverted auxiliary overwhelming the introverted dominant (see discussion of 'Introverted Complexity No. 47' on p. 52). For example, in my case, intuition says 'Let's look at the concept of "Preference" – there are lots of relevant ideas: there's "instinctive drift", the A/B/C model of intelligence, self-actualization, aptitude versus attainment, and that's just for a start'. And feeling replies 'I can see you find that exciting, but it's too much for me. I want a book that selects the best bits and that I don't feel swamped by'. And intuition argues back, seductively, 'But some of the best bits might be in the ideas I've mentioned'.

The particular skirmish and the general tension are best resolved, according to type theory, by my dominant function having the last word, either at this point or soon. If I were an ENFP or an INFJ then N would be my dominant, with Feeling playing a secondary role, and N should, in theory, dominate. However, an ENFP or INFJ with insufficient development of F would tend to include too many things and not reach closure. There is a balance to find.

Other factors are involved in writing, of course, and the conflict described above could be interpreted in other ways. What type theory does, though, is suggest a different solution for each type, describe both elements of personality positively and underline the role of balance in gathering information and coming to conclusions.

CONCLUSIONS

1. Type theory spells out radically different styles of studying, teaching and writing effectively. It suggests emphasizing a person's own style (stemming in theory mainly from their dominant function) and then adding elements of the other styles.
2. 'Type is a strategy for improving education that does not change content fields, produce additional paperwork, or require that changes be made rapidly' (Murphy, 1992, p. 91).

Type and organizations

Many of the topics discussed in other chapters are relevant to organizations, e.g. counselling (Chapter 7) and MBTI training (Chapter 10). The success or otherwise of employee selection, appraisal, career development and job design depends in part on an understanding of personality and motivation. This chapter focuses on occupations, in particular the idea of the 'good manager' and the place of the MBTI and type theory in selection. It also touches on communication and stress management.

OCCUPATIONS

Many factors are involved in a person's choice of occupation, including advice, fashion, availability and luck. Personality also plays a part and people of each type tend to find some activities, and therefore some occupations and careers, more fulfilling than others. See, for example, the basic motives associated with each dominant function (Table 3.5), Tables 9.1 and 9.2 in this chapter and the numerous tables relating type and occupations in Myers and McCaulley (1985).

All occupations so far studied have different proportions of types (taking into account the proportions in the general population) consistent with type theory. For example, the arts are particularly attractive to NFs, production management to STJs and so on. However, it is important to add that people whose types do not in theory make them appropriate for a particular kind of work may still do it well and, indeed, make an unusual contribution because they are different from the majority of their colleagues. On the other hand, it is also possible that some are unhappy misfits. A further qualification is that some work, e.g. management (discussed below), can be carried out with equal effectiveness in a variety of ways, each consistent with a different psychological type.

Tables 9.1 and 9.2 illustrate the general finding. Business students' MBTI types are predominantly TJ (63%) and NT (46%) and counsellors are predominantly NFs (56%). There are enough data on type and occupation to list the top and bottom ten occupations for each type, with samples of at least 50 people in each occupation (Macdaid, 1988). For example, ESTJs tend to choose careers in management and the police and not journalism, the arts or counselling. There are differences within occupations too, e.g. ISTPs tend to be police officers but not detectives. More generally, the TJ types tend to choose careers of 'power and authority' and FPs tend to avoid them.

Table 9.1: MBTI types (%) of postgraduate students in business administration (N=228) (simplified from Myers and McCaulley, 1985, Table 4.5)

ISTJ 21	ISFJ 3	INFJ 1	INTJ 14
ISTP 6	ISFP 0	INFP 1	INTP 10
ESTP 2	ESFP 0	ENFP 3	ENTP 8
ESTJ 14	ESFJ 1	ENFJ 1	ENTJ 14

However, there are problems with the data on type and occupation. First, they are based on MBTI types rather than verified types and some research, e.g. Kummerow (1988), has found some false (and judicious) completing of the MBTI in organizational settings, for obvious reasons. Second, there is some overlap: all the types can be found in all occupations. Hammer (1991) examined the overlap criticism in detail. He found no overlap between the top 20 occupations for ISTJs and ENFPs, 5% overlap between ISTJs and INTJs and 45% overlap between ISTJs and ESTJs. Further, type and temperament theory predict more overlap between STJs as a subtype than ITJs as a subgroup; SN is seen as the single most influential preference in occupational choice (Myers, 1980) and SJ and NT are different temperaments. Hammer's analysis then provides impressive evidence for the validity of type theory and the MBTI in terms of occupational choice and against the overlap criticism.

A third problem is that the relationship between type and occupation needs investigating at a more refined level: we need more evidence on occupation,

Table 9.2: MBTI types (%) of counsellors (N=359) (simplified from Myers and McCaulley, 1985, Table 4.9)

ISTJ 6	ISFJ 6	INFJ 8	INTJ 3
ISTP 1	ISFP 4	INFP 14	INTP 2
ESTP 1	ESFP 6	ENFP 23	ENTP 3
ESTJ 5	ESFJ 7	ENFJ 11	ENTJ 2

type, competence and 'job satisfaction' (or job 'excitement' or 'fulfilment'). Scarbrough's (1993) study of job satisfaction and type in accountants illustrates some of the complexities of this area of research. Forty two per cent of his sample of 255 accountants were female. Most of the sample had 4–7 years' experience in their profession. Scarbrough found that 85% of the male accountants and 46% of the females reported as Ts on the MBTI, that the most frequently occurring types were ISTJ (20%) and ESTJ (15%) and the least, ISFP (1%), INFP (2%) and ESFP (2%). These percentages are consistent with previous research on accountants' psychological type. As for job satisfaction, there were not enough participants of most of the types (despite the large sample) to allow statistical tests. Only five types could be compared and these (on an 18-item, 6-point scale, from 'very dissatisfied' to 'very satisfied') were not significantly different. The major effect was from gender. For example, there were no overall differences on job satisfaction between Es and Is, but E men and I women both reported higher levels of satisfaction than I men and E women.

For careers counsellors, the data on type and occupation provide a framework for exploring reasons for career choices and interests. Macdaid also suggests clients interviewing someone of the same type to themselves working in the particular occupation. For research, I think interviews with rare types in particular occupations, e.g. the three ISFPs in Scarbrough's sample (assuming they really are ISFPs) would be worthwhile, to clarify their true types and explore their likes and dislikes about their work, any 'niche' they might have found and whether they saw themselves as different from the majority of their colleagues. Some of the ISTJs and ESTJs should also be interviewed, as a comparison group, and to explore how they actually use their dominant and auxiliary functions in their work.

Temperament theory (Keirsey and Bates, 1978), here as elsewhere, provides a potential shortcut: it is simpler and therefore loses information, but it is also easier to apply. The suggested relationships between temperament and occupations are broadly as shown in Table 9.3. The suggested underlying motives were indicated in Table 3.7 (p. 58).

Table 9.3: Temperament and occupations (examples) (adapted from Myers and McCaulley, 1985)

SP	SJ	NT	NF
Performers	Managers	Scientists	Counsellors
Entrepreneurs	Accountants	Architects	Journalists
Troubleshooters	Police	Engineers	Artists
One-person businesses	Dentists	Designers	Psychologists
Rescue teams	Teachers	Managers	Clergy

Each temperament has a part to play in any organization: SPs to solve immediate problems, SJs to organize and for stability, NTs to develop models and consider the long term, NFs to help morale. For example, 55% of clergy (all denominations) are NFs, as are 54% of teachers of art, music and drama, 51% of artists and writers, 48% of psychologists, 46% of journalists and so on, compared with about 18% of NFs in the general population. Conversely, 4% of farmers and 4% of the police are NFs (all these figures derived from MBTI types – Myers and McCaulley, 1985). At the level of type, 31% of steelworkers, 22% of dentists, 20% of accountants but only 4% of writers and journalists and 3% of psychologists are ISTJs.

THE 'GOOD MANAGER'

Managers, at least in the USA, UK and Japan, tend to be the toughminded ISTJs, ESTJs, INTJs and ENTJs (Myers and McCaulley, 1985; Walck, 1992b; Reynierse, 1993). Type theory, though, is very clear that a good manager may be of any of the types; that type development matters much more than type itself; and that type tends to affect style rather than effectiveness of management. '"What type is the best ...?" is always the wrong question' (McCaulley, 1992, p.1). McCaulley suggested what she sees as some more useful questions:

1. What types are frequent or rare in leadership positions?
2. Which leadership tasks come most easily to each type? Which are difficult or distasteful?
3. In what leadership setting is each type most likely to be more successful? Less successful?

She suggests that the best managers both have good type development and recognize the value of all the other preferences, in themselves, in others or both. However, Hogan *et al.* (1994) argue that the effectiveness of leaders should be evaluated in terms of their team's performance and that good leaders (my translation from their Big Five terms) are generally ENFJs.

Hirsh and Kummerow (1990) provide the most concise and plausible descriptions of styles of leadership but these have not so far been systematically tested in a direct way. They are based firmly on type theory and are thus quite well supported indirectly (Chs 2 and 3). However, although most of the descriptions are true by definition, e.g. ESTJ managers tend to be 'Quick to decide' (p.19), a few are more arguable, e.g. ESTJs tend to be 'Crisp and direct at getting to the core of the situation' (p. 18). I would say that perceptions of 'core' will vary. In any case, plausibility and indirect evidence are not enough.

Table 9.4 uses temperament theory to illustrate the general 'flavour' of type's approach to leadership style (see also Table 3.7). The strengths of each temperament can also be liabilities; much depends on the organization and on the political and social context. For example, SJs are seen as the 'backbone' of an organization and successful organizations in a stable economy need SJ strengths to consolidate and grow. However, the procedures can become too important or even ends in themselves or the context can change; then NT strengths become more necessary if the organization is to survive. Moreover, within these broad considerations, organizations are seen as likely to be at their best with a blend and balance of the four temperaments, if this can be achieved.

Table 9.4: Temperament and leadership/management style (simplified from Hirsh and Kummerow, 1990, Keirsey and Bates, 1978, and Brownsword, 1987)

	Likely strengths	**Possible problems**
SP	Troubleshooting, responding to crises now and flexibly, negotiating	Details, routine, long-range planning
SJ	Stability, consolidation, procedures, responsibility	Change, uncertainty
NT	Vision, designing new systems, high standards	Emotional problems, consolidating, lots of crises, appreciating
NF	Support, encouragement, clarity about values	Focusing on the task, being objective

A useful exercise is to ask managers to each write a story about their 'ideal organization' or to choose from descriptions (Hirsh, 1992). Then groups of STs, SFs, NTs and NFs devise or choose a 'group story' and relate it to the whole group. Usually there are marked contrasts. For example, STs tend to emphasize control, bureaucracy and hierarchy; SFs warm, human aspects; NTs broad issues and new ideas and markets; and NFs broad issues and human ideals, development of self and others more than duty or power (see Lawrence, 1993, p. 196 and his Chapter 12 on introducing type into an organization).

Employee selection

The MBTI itself is not appropriate as a selection measure because it is not intended to measure abilities or performance and because it actually does not measure them in any straightforward way (Walck, 1992b). Other personality measures have useful, but not strong, relationships with effectiveness at work (see, for example, Robertson and Kinder 1993). Moreover, the MBTI is an easy questionnaire to fake and for most jobs the desired qualities are obvious (or the applicant thinks they are, which is just as unhelpful).

Type **theory**, on the other hand, can be very useful in selection. It can clarify the qualities needed to do the particular job, suggest lines of questioning and ability tests to use in selection for it and work against 'cloning' – the tendency to recruit the same kind of person as the selector. Moreover, some methods of selection will suit some types more than others, introducing an unfair source of discrimination. The MBTI is best used before selection, e.g. in designing application forms (Flock and Bayne, 1990), and after selection, e.g. in team building (Kummerow and McAllister, 1988).

When 'cloning' occurs in organizations, or at a particular level of an organization, that organization tends to have the associated strengths and weaknesses of the particular type. For example, Kroeger and Thuesen (1992, pp. 85–6) described a practice of six dentists who were all of the same psychological type. They were very skilful and efficient but they found fewer and fewer people were coming to see them. They worked harder, but even fewer people came. They worked out that efficiency was not enough; their business needed other skills, ones which did not come easily to them. The choice at this point is between development – someone taking responsibility for the neglected aspects of their work (in this case E and F skills (see Chapter 4) – or selecting someone new who has those skills already.

COMMUNICATION

A major aim of type theory, noted early in Chapter 1, is to encourage the 'constructive use of differences'. In particular, it can explain, at least in part, attractions and conflicts between people and the strengths and weaknesses of particular groups (as in the dental practice described above). Table 9.5 suggests some of the most likely problems between people with each preference and some strategies for trying to prevent or manage them. The strategies may seem to be expressed rather grudgingly in the table; type theory can lead to a greater appreciation of differences, as well as increasing understanding and tolerance of them.

Table 9.5: The preferences, some communication problems and some communication strategies (modified from Bayne, 1993)

The most likely problems (according to theory) include:

Between E and I	:	contact v time alone
Between S and N	:	details and realism v general picture and speculation
Between T and F	:	seen as unsympathetic and critical v illogical and too agreeable
Between J and P	:	decisive and controlling v flexible and changeable (or 'pushy' v 'wishy-washy')

Some strategies are:

E	→	I	Allow time for privacy and to reflect
I	→	E	Explain need for time, allow for other's need too talk in order to clarify
S	→	N	Overall picture first, with relevant details
N	→	S	Say a particular idea is half-formed and/or include relevant detail
T	→	F	Include effects on people, begin with points of agreement
F	→	T	Include reasons and consequences, be brief
J	→	P	Allow for some flexibility in plans, style of working, etc. and the other's need not to be controlled
P	→	J	Allow for some planning and structure and for the other's need to control and decide

---

c.f. Table 7.5

For example, Ts can see Fs as too soft and personal but can reframe this as a warm concern for people's morale and for harmony. On the other hand, Fs can see Ts as too cold and detached but can reframe this as a useful concern for analysis and for improvement as a result of criticism. Although constructively using difference in this way can be very difficult, it is possible. A complication is that some conflicts occur despite similarity in type – for example, two Fs with a clash of values. Moreover, applying type to communication can be quite subtle, e.g. after an MBTI course, a thinking manager began to compliment her feeling staff on their work; her staff, however, were less pleased than she hoped, because Fs tend to appreciate being complimented for their personal qualities more than their work.

Table 9.5 is at the level of the preferences but can also apply most to dominant functions or possibly to the function which is used most in the outside world, e.g. T in ISTJs. Kirby (1992) gave the following example of a conflict explained by type dynamics rather than preferences: an INFP and an ENFP found that when they planned a project together or tried to solve a problem, the ENFP would find the INFP reaching a conclusion before the ENFP wanted to. Moreover, the F conclusion would often appear suddenly – at least to the ENFP. This did not seem to be an EI difference; indeed, EI on its own would suggest the I exploring in more depth. Type dynamics, though, suggests that the conflict was between extraverted N and introverted F. See Quenk (1993) for discussion of type dynamics and most introductions to type for discussions of communication (e.g. Kroeger and Thuesen, 1988; Murray and Murray, 1988).

Percival *et al.* (1992) related preferences and combinations of preferences to five modes of handling conflict. The combinations were the most fruitful, with ETJs (i.e. dominant T) reporting that they competed – 'It has to be my way'; EFJs (dominant F) that they collaborated – 'Let's see if we can find a solution that satisfies all parties'; ETPs (dominant S or N) and ITPs that they compromised – 'Let's split the difference'; and all introverted combinations except ITPs that they avoided – 'I don't want to deal with this'. The fifth mode was to accommodate: 'I agree'. SN was not related to reported mode. A strength of the study was that the same results were found in two quite different groups (of 160 and 180 people respectively).

Team-building is an obvious application of the MBTI. Kummerow and McAllister (1988) discussed several case studies of their approach to team building, which includes the notion of a 'team type' (the most frequent preferences) and the strengths and weaknesses suggested by it. The relationship or contrast between the leader's type and the team's can also be influential. The emphasis, of course, is on developing trust, valuing differences and consciously applying the idea of type development.

STRESS

Type theory suggests that radically different aspects of work (and life outside work) are likely to be experienced as enjoyable or stressful by each type and that the characteristic reactions to stress of the types also differ. Tables 9.6 and 9.7 illustrate these ideas for the four temperaments. As a workshop exercise, they work consistently well but they have not been formally tested yet. Another obvious further step is to propose and test relationships between type and coping strategies.

As with other applications of type theory and the MBTI, the links are direct and clear: SJs tend, by definition, to like security more than people of the other temperaments do and therefore to feel threatened by change, especially when the change is sudden or major. The other types, especially NPs and above all ENTPs and ENFPs, are more likely to thrive on (and create) change. On a personal level, you may like to ask (1) 'What do I find most stressful?' and (2) 'Does it relate to my type?'.

Table 9.6: Temperament and most liked aspects of work (from Nicolson and Bayne, 1990)

SP	Emergencies and pressures. Solving practical problems, perhaps in a high-risk, tense environment. Variety, a lot going on. 'Adaptable realists'
SJ	Meeting deadlines, resolving issues and problems in a structured and stable environment. Attending to details. Planning well in advance. To be socially concerned and accepted. Security. 'Realistic decision-makers'
NT	Producing new high-quality ideas. Being respected for their ideas and achievements by people they respect. Autonomy. 'Logical and ingenious'
NF	Helping others in a 'nurturing' way. Being a resource. Being approved of and supported in a stimulating and harmonious environment. Making full use of own talents. Being 'energized through accomplishment'. 'Enthusiastic and insightful'

Table 9.7: Temperament, stressful aspects of work, and reactions to stress (adapted from unpublished work by Valerie Stewart, from Nicolson and Bayne, 1990)

Stressful aspects

SP	Not much happening. Monotony. Unclear or no information. Lack of freedom. (Unclear objectives matter much less)
SJ	Unclear objectives. Changes of plan. Ambiguity. Lack of control
NT	Doing routine and repetitive things, especially if they're detailed as well. Bureaucracy. Difficult relationships
NF	Conflict. Saying no. Depressed and suicidal people. Criticism

Reactions to stress

SP	Frivolity, flight, 'go own way', breakdown
SJ	Redefine objectives, more resources, double check, more control, dogmatic
NT	Overwork, fight, intolerance, conform rebelliously, pedantic debate
NF	Self-sacrifice, cynicism, hysteria, depression

Some ideas about stress seem to be generally true, e.g. that the effects can gather surreptitiously, that it is therefore effective (but difficult) to notice early warning signals and that in many occupations there is always more to do and that not recognizing this – and taking appropriate action – is likely to lead to too much stress. One generally effective way of coping with too much stress, based on type theory, may be to use your dominant function, e.g. for T or F to finish off something (or something other than a frustrating problem), make some decisions or make a list, and for S or N to start a different activity.

Table 9.8 suggests some coping methods. The principle underlying the column headed 'What they need' is to use that preference when under stress and, generally, to behave like yourself more of the time. The principle underlying 'A good stretch' is that sometimes the most effective strategy is to seek balance by using the opposite preference, though perhaps only briefly (Kroeger with Thuesen, 1992, p. 247). Obviously, the recommendations in Table 9.8 can be seen as trying to 'have it both ways'; however, I think they recognize the complexities of type and particularly type development.

Table 9.8: Stress and coping (modified from Kroeger with Thuesen, 1992)

What they need	'A good stretch'
E To talk (with others)	Take notes, write in a journal
I To reflect	Intimate, spontaneous talk
S A sensory activity	Fantasize
N To design something new	Do something sensory/detailed
T To feel competent, to analyse and challenge	Empathize
F Harmony	Analyse
J A plan or finishing something	Abandon the schedule
P Flexibility and autonomy	Stick to a (sub)plan

If you are interested in finding out more on strategies for coping with stress, see Bayne *et al.* (1994) and Bond (1986). For a review of research on methods of coping, see Rosenthal (1993).

Type offers a two-stage model of reactions to stress. Initially the person becomes an increasingly extreme and caricatured version of their normal self, as shown for the temperaments in the second part of Table 9.7. Then, if the stress continues, it is suggested that they 'flip' into the fourth function and again a negative caricature of it. The results of this proposed second stage are outlined in Table 9.9.

Kopp (1974) and Quenk (1993) offer further observations on stress and type, which are mainly consistent with Table 9.9. Kopp, for example, suggests that ISTJs and ISFJs respond to great stress with suspiciousness and 'morbid fantasies', but also that their 'best protection' is a 'somewhat zany, semi-whimsical viewing of the world as something of a comic charade' (p. 117).

Odeluga (1993) interviewed 25 people about stress, all of whom had either thinking or feeling as their dominant function (the interviewer did not know which, but may have been able to judge – see Chapter 6). He asked them first about their experience of everyday stress in detail and then about 'a time when

Table 9.9: Type and reactions to a high level of stress (adapted from Hirsh and Kummerow, 1990, from Bayne, 1994, Table 2)

Type	Fourth function	Reaction
ISTJ ISFJ ESFP ESTP	N	See very gloomy possibilities or feel doomed and trapped
INTJ INFJ ENFP ENTP	S	Overdo something, e.g. make lots of long lists, overeat or behave obsessively in some other way
INTP ISTP ESTJ ENTJ	F	Emotional outbursts or feel isolated and unloved
ISFP INFP ESFJ ENFJ	T	Lots of analysing or very critical or feel useless and incompetent

they were feeling very stressed'. Finally, they put three of the four reactions to extreme stress listed in Table 9.9 in rank order.

Nineteen of the 25 participants chose T or F fourth function responses rather than S or N ones, but not in the pattern predicted by the model. The qualitative data were strikingly supportive but not systematically reported, so selective memory or other forms of bias are obvious hazards (as they are for the accuracy of the model itself). Nevertheless, a further test seems worthwhile.

There is some fairly clear empirical evidence for both the escalation part of the type and stress model (Stage One) and the flipping over (Stage Two). Van Denburg and Kiesler (1993) studied what they called 'transactional escalation' in a high stress interview. They found that the interviewees' typical behaviour became more intense and more rigid under greater stress. However, their study was restricted to one kind of person, described as 'friendly-submissive'. In research relevant to Stage Two of the model, Garden (1985, 1988) found that 'burnout' produced symptoms which were 'a loss of the attributes typically expected of that type' (1988, p. 13). Moreover, she noted an increase, in some instances, in the characteristics associated with the opposite type, e.g. thinking types showing higher levels of concern for others.

Garden's research on type and burnout is complicated and needs replicating and extending. In my view it was carefully done, the results are practically as well as statistically significant (some of the 1985 results are presented using each person as the unit of analysis) and it provides quite good evidence for type's model of stress. It may also – indirectly – be evidence for some aspects of type dynamics but the research was not designed for this purpose and the analysis does not distinguish between dominant and auxiliary functions.

Time management

A central element of the JP preference seems to be attitude towards time, either seeking to control it (J) or adapt to it (P). This idea on its own may be a useful way of responding to many time management problems. The main application of type theory to time management is, however, a familiar one: if you are a J, add some P qualities while remaining essentially a J and vice versa for Ps (Kroeger with Thuesen, 1992).

Courses in time management tend to be ESTJ and ENTJ in orientation, with lots of emphasis on drawing up plans and writing lists. In contrast to the 'one right way' approach, Lewis and Lowe (1992) have proposed relationships between the functions and different time management skills (pp. 67–70). As noted earlier, the general principle is to apply your own preferences (and perhaps the dominant function and J or P particularly). I find their general idea exciting but the specific applications and rationales hard to summarize. Therefore I will include my understanding of their recommendations for Ps only. They are as follows: throw your watch away, change your routines continually, work in different rooms, alternate activities, work with your natural rhythms and values. Get these conditions right and you will get things done in the outside world 'naturally and effortlessly'. I hope this notion is true. It may, of course, seem crazy to people who do not prefer P.

CONCLUSIONS

1. Type is related to choice of occupation, though some occupations – for example, management – may be most usefully seen in terms of style and type development rather than as most suited to a particular type.
2. Type theory is useful in selection but generally the MBTI is not. Indeed, its use and misuse in selection may detract from its role in training and development.
3. Further research on people who in theory are in the 'wrong' job for their type but who are effective and enjoy their work, and on type's model of stress, seems particularly worthwhile.

10	# Introductory MBTI workshops: some ideas and exercises

I have written this chapter mainly for MBTI trainers. I suggest three ideas or principles to consider when introducing the MBTI in a workshop and discuss two issues: when to complete and score the MBTI itself (before or during the workshop) and how in general terms to interpret the results. Finally, I outline the best exercises I have found so far for showing type in action. I do not attempt to discuss the many possible ways of designing a workshop or to provide a trainer's manual. (Hirsh (1992) contains scripts and other supporting materials as well as more than 40 exercises.) The ideas or principles I would like to suggest are:

1. try to prevent negative reactions;
2. appropriate simplicity (don't overload);
3. trust the process.

The rest of the chapter organizes the exercises in five sections: preferences; temperament; type dynamics; type development; specific applications. For other exercises, see Hirsh (1992), Lawrence (1993), Kroeger and Thuesen (1988, 1992, 1994), and earlier chapters of this book.

THREE PRINCIPLES

Try to prevent negative reactions

The 'atmosphere' in a workshop is ideally a trusting, open one, which includes freedom to be critical, so I do not mean 'try to make everything sweet and harmonious'. The following steps can be helpful in anticipating criticisms and thus preventing some of them. First, what the participants have been told beforehand about the workshop and you, the contract between you and the group, and your introduction, play a part. Recently, as part of my introduction, I have said 'Type may sound like stereotyping, putting people in boxes. I see it as a step towards understanding individuality, not an attempt to capture it whole. That's a misuse of type'. This usually disarms, at least to some extent, concern about boxes or categorization.

I have also found that introducing the concept of preference early allows an economical and positive answer to some comments. For example, if someone says 'I behave differently in different situations' you can point to the results of the handedness exercise (outlined in the next section) if they are on display. I nearly always do the handedness exercise (Table 1.2, p. 4) **before** participants complete the MBTI.

Appropriate simplicity

It can be very tempting to tell course members all the best bits about type that you know. I try to hold back and go more at their pace. Kroeger (1991) made this idea more concrete: 'Never do dominant and auxiliary in a one day or less session'. I think it is better to do one or two pairs of preferences in a session, with a very brief outline of other elements, than to try to squeeze everything in.

Trust the process

The phrase 'trust the process' was used by Kroeger (1991). He meant that the way groups go about exercises can be at least as revealing as the products of those exercises and that it is a good idea to ask the group to report on their 'process' (if this is too much a piece of jargon, you can ask 'What is/was it like to be in your group?', 'How did you go about the task?'). Also, press for detail if necessary; a word like 'practical' or 'autonomous' – perhaps most words – can be used very differently by different groups. Similarly, even if two groups of different types behave in the same way, their reasons can be very different. I think trusting the process is a particularly good strategy when an exercise 'fails' to produce output supporting type or when the output contradicts it, but it is very useful more routinely too.

One or two observers, perhaps people who are unsure about doing the exercise, are another source of information. The contrast between groups doing the same exercise is sometimes dramatic and unfortunately seen by too few people. I also suggest to individuals who seem uncomfortable in their group, or to the whole group, that they see what the other groups are like and whether they feel more 'at home' in one of them than the others. Or you can ask a T and an F (say) to observe a TF exercise. There is a risk that their MBTI preference results will be wrong (at this stage they are unverified) but choosing people with very clear results reduces this risk (see also Chapter 6).

I like exercises which are very simple to set up and I think that discussing the outcomes is at least as important as the exercise itself. I also like to change details of the exercises and their number during a workshop, depending on such factors as time and whether an exercise is working or not, but I realize (not least from the reactions of co-leaders!) that this is the best way for me and not for others.

My approach to analysing the outcomes of an exercise is to be flexible within a broad framework of observations from participants on content and process, with comments from me if necessary. But if the exercise has failed to demonstrate type in its content, I ask about process first or go straight into another exercise on the same aspect of type in the hope that it will work better. This degree of flexibility does not suit some trainers or participants and I do modify my style for the predominant type in a group (but see Chapter 8 on teaching style).

ISSUES

When to complete the MBTI

There are two distinct views here. One is that ideally participants complete the MBTI before the workshop. Then the workshop leader can do the scoring beforehand and take MBTI types into account in designing the workshop, and there is more time during the workshop for exercises, etc. Kroeger (1991) expressed this view strongly, adding that consultants are not paid to watch people fill in questionnaires and that participants tend to make errors when scoring their own MBTIs.

The second view is that there is more 'ownership' of the results if people complete their own questionnaires knowing they will also be scoring them. They may also be more likely to complete them accurately once they have seen the workshop leader and clarified any doubts (the opposite may also be true), and the leader can respond to any doubts and queries about the questionnaire. Moreover, participants seem to enjoy learning the scoring (and the scoring keys are beautifully designed). I do the scoring as a cascade, i.e. I show the first four to finish how to use the scoring keys on their own answer sheets and they show the others, with me supervising. I look at each set of results to see if it looks accurate (I typically work with groups of 20–30). If it looks suspect I rescore it myself, tactfully. The one-to-one contact (in my style of leading a workshop) also tends to contribute to an atmosphere of trust.

With students (psychology and counselling), I have found it essential, when they are scoring their own answer sheets, to say firmly something like 'Some people tend to go straight in and not to read instructions. Please have a go at reading them **one at a time** and doing **each one in turn**'. I go round, of course, and check/help. Generally, students take longer than manual workers to complete the scoring.

Interpretation of MBTI results

Again, there are two distinct views (with variations). The first is that information about type should be given before the MBTI results are known, so that participants can make provisional choices for each preference and therefore their type. The advantage is that the MBTI results then take their place later as a further piece of evidence.

The second approach is to say in effect 'I'd like to let what the letters mean emerge from the exercises (if they work) and to tell you more about the letters as we go along, with written descriptions near the end'. The advantage is that the outcomes of the exercises (assuming no prior knowledge of type) cannot be biased by information about type. I ask the group to complete a group type table – prominently marked PROVISIONAL MBTI TYPES, with the day's date. This usually leads to a useful discussion which can be added to by asking, before the scoring and for each person's own eyes alone, predictions about which people are 'most like you' and 'least like you' in the group. It also gives the leader a good opportunity to underline the provisional nature of the MBTI results.

This second approach is more participative than Jeffries' (1991) for example, who recommended the following 'ideal sequence':

1. some general observations about type and the MBTI;
2. an overview of the eight preferences – 'This section is at the heart of the presentation. I routinely discuss the eight preferences for about two hours, grounding the entire time in anecdotes ...' (p. 74);
3. return participants' results;
4. exercises;
5. type table;
6. more input;
7. warnings.

EXERCISES

The concept of preference

The handedness exercise is standard in type workshops and was discussed earlier (see Table 1.2, p. 4). A complementary or alternative exercise is as follows. I developed the exercise as a concrete, active start for groups of manual workers (Bayne, 1992). However, the exercise works well with psychology students and counsellors/health professionals too.

Step 1: I ask something like: 'What kinds of people are there? Give me some words?' and write four or five of the group's terms on a flipchart.

One group of manual workers suggested first the term 'Plonker'. The second term was 'Dreamer', the third 'Generous', and so on.

Step 2: 'What are some opposites for these words?' The opposite for 'Plonker' was 'Cool Dude' and for 'Dreamer', 'Realist', for 'Generous', 'Cold' and 'Mean', and so on.

Step 3: I suggest:

1. that usually there is a positive word and a negative one in each pair and that this is not so in psychological type or for the MBTI;
2. that people usually do both things, but that one is more characteristic, e.g. no-one is a Cool Dude all the time, in all circumstances;
3. that psychological type/MBTI is concerned with four of the main ways in which people's personalities are different.

The EI preference

First, four general points:

1. Some of these exercises can be tried with combinations of preferences, e.g. EI and JP (giving four groups) or EI and SN (four groups) or groups can be divided on a single preference using the number part of the MBTI results, e.g. E 45–33 might be one group, E 31–17 another, and so on. Generally I make the I groups a little smaller than the E groups.
2. A follow-up to any of the following exercises is to ask each group to think of good qualities about (a) their own preference and (b) the opposite preference. Sometimes it is also valuable to ask about dislikes and difficulties and for questions each group would like to ask the other. (Allow time for the groups to prepare.)
3. Precise wording seems to be important, more for some exercises than others.
4. I sometimes say 'stop' after a minute or so and ask each group to make a note of what their group has done so far and their first reactions to the exercise.

Suggested exercises for EI

● When you see someone you'd like to know better, what do you do?
● What is your first reaction to being given an essay topic?

The SN preference

● Describe time. One (high scoring) N group produced a single word answer: 'Sand'. However, N groups usually write a lot of answers to this question and S groups are briefer and more concrete.
● Describe this room. (TF can 'interfere' with the outcome, so ST, SF, NT, NF groups may be best.)
● Describe the first part of your day.

The TF preference

● Present a moral dilemma and ask for a decision and a basis for the decision.
● Ask 'What is love?' or 'power' or 'conflict' (probably many other words

would be effective, but these are particularly meaningful for Ts and Fs). I enjoyed one group of Ts' frustration with being asked to stop discussing a definition of love: 'We were just getting our teeth into it'.

● You are walking in a wood and find an injured animal. How do you react?

The JP preference

● What is really important about plans and planning?

This is my most reliable exercise and often I start with it, even though the most obvious preferences to explore first are EI (the first pair of preferences) or SN (the first pair of functions). When the exercise works well, the high J and low J groups set about the task with energy, list lots of things that are really important about plans and focus on the task. The 'purest' outcome for the high P group – which happens – is that they present a blank sheet.

Temperament

A particularly reliable exercise is to ask 'What is most rewarding about work?' and to use Table 9.6 as a handout.

Type development

See Chapter 4.

Specific applications

In education, see Murphy (1992) and Lawrence (1993). In organizations generally, see Hirsh (1992) and Kroeger and Thuesen (1988, 1992).

Appendix: Addresses for training, membership and publications

For training and publications in UK

Oxford Psychologists Press,
Lambourne House,
311–21 Banbury Road,
Oxford OX2 7JH
Phone: 01865 510203
Fax: 01865 310368

For training and publications in USA

CAPT (Center for Applications of Psychological Type),
2720 NW 6th Street,
Gainesville,
FL 32609
Phone: 800 777-2248
Fax: 904 378-0503

Otto Kroeger Associates,
3605 Chain Bridge Road,
Fairfax,
VA 22030
Phone: 703 591-6284
Fax: 703 591-8338

Type and Temperament Inc.
Box 200,
Gladwyne,
PA 19035-0200
Phone: 610 527-2330
Fax: 610 527-1722

Membership organization (UK)

BAPT (British Association for Psychological Type),
Emmaus House,
Clifton,
Bristol BS8 4PD
Phone: 01272 738056
Fax: 01272 239508

Membership organization (USA)

APT (Association for Psychological Type),
9140 Ward Parkway,
Kansas City,
MO 64114
Phone: 816 444-3500

Journal of Psychological Type

Dr Tom Carskadon,
Department of Psychology,
Mississippi State University,
PO Box 6161,
MS 39762
Phone: 601 325-7655

The Type Reporter

In the UK from Oxford Psychologists Press (above).
In the USA from:
The Type Reporter Inc.,
524 North Paxton Street,
Alexandria,
VA 22304
Phone: 703 823-3730

References

Ahadi, S. and Diener, E. (1989) Multiple determinants and effect size. *Journal of Personality and Social Psychology*, **56** (3), 398–406.

Allinson, T., Cooper, C.L. and Reynolds, P. (1989) Stress counselling in the workplace. The Post Office experience. *The Psychologist*, **2** (9), 384–8.

Allport, G.W. (1953) The trend in motivational theory. *American Journal of Orthopsychiatry*, **23**, 107–19.

Allport, G.W. (1961a) *Pattern and Growth in Personality*, Holt, London.

Allport, G.W. (1961b) Comment, in *Existential Psychology* (ed. R. May), Random House, New York.

Ambady, N. and Rosenthal, R. (1993) Half a minute: teacher evaluations from thin slices of nonverbal behaviour and physical attractiveness. *Journal of Personality and Social Psychology*, **64** (3), 431–41.

Barger, N. and Kirby, L. (1993) The interaction of cultural values and type development: INTP women across cultures. *Bulletin of Psychological Type*, **16** (4), 14–16.

Barkham, M. (1993) Understanding, implementing and presenting counselling evaluation, in *Counselling and Psychology for Health Professionals* (eds R. Bayne and P. Nicolson), Chapman & Hall, London.

Barrett-Lennard, G.T. (1993) The phases and focus of empathy. *British Journal of Medical Psychology*, **66**, 3–14.

Bayne, R. (1977) The meaning and measurement of self-disclosure. *British Journal of Guidance and Counselling*, **5**, 159–66.

Bayne, R. (1988a) Accuracy in judging the four attitudes. *Journal of Psychological Type*, **16**, 61–6.

Bayne, R. (1988b) Psychological type as a model of personality development. *British Journal of Guidance and Counselling*, **16** (2), 167–75.

Bayne, R. (1992) Introducing type experientially. *Bulletin of Psychological Type*, **15** (3), 11–12.

Bayne, R. (1993) Psychological type, conversations and counselling, in *Counselling and Psychology for Health Professionals* (eds R. Bayne and P. Nicolson), Chapman & Hall, London.

Bayne, R. (1994) The Myers–Briggs versus the 'Big Five'. *The Psychologist*, **7** (1), 14–16.

Bayne, R. (in press) Psychological type and counselling. *British Journal of Guidance and Counselling*.

Bayne, R. and O'Neill, F. (1988) Handwriting and personality: an empirical test of expert graphologists' judgements. *Guidance and Assessment Review*, **4** (4), 1–3.

Bayne, R., Horton, I., Merry, T. and Noyes, E. (1994) *The Counsellor's Handbook, A practical A–Z guide to professional and clinical practice*, Chapman & Hall, London.

Bergeman, C.S., Chipuer, H.M., Plomin, R. *et al.* (1993) Genetic and environmental effects on openness to experience, agreeableness, and conscientiousness: an adoption/twin study. *Journal of Personality*, **61** (2), 159–79.

Berry, D.S. and Finch Wero, J.L. (1993) Accuracy in face perception: a view from ecological psychology. *Journal of Personality*, **61** (4), 497–520.

Boice, R. (1987) A program for facilitating scholarly writing. *Higher Education Research and Development*, **6** (1), 9–20.

Bond, M. (1986) *Stress and Self-Awareness: A Guide for Nurses*, Heinemann, London.

Borkenau, P. and Liebler, A. (1992) Trait inferences: sources of validity at zero acquaintance. *Journal of Personality and Social Psychology*, **62** (4), 645–57.

Bouchard, T.J., Lykken, D.T., McGue, M., Segal, N.L. and Tellegen, A. (1990) Sources of human psychological differences: the Minnesota study of twins raised apart. *Science*, **250**, 223–8.

Brammer, L.M., Abrego, P.J. and Shostrom, E. (1993) *Therapeutic Counseling and Psychotherapy*, 6th edn, Prentice-Hall, Englewood Cliffs.

Briggs, K.C. (1926) Meet yourself: how to use the personality paint box. Reprinted in *MBTI News* (1981), **4** (1), 1, 8–10.

Brownell, K.D. (1991) Dieting and the search for the perfect body: where physiology and culture collide. *Behaviour Therapy*, **22**, 1–12.

Brownell, K.D. and Rodin, J. (1994) The dieting maelstrom. Is it possible and advisable to lose weight? *American Psychologist*, **49** (9), 781–91.

Brownsword, A. (1987) *It Takes All Types*! Baytree Publication Co., Fairfax, CA.

Carlson, J.G. (1985) Recent assessments of the MBTI. *Journal of Personality Assessment*, **49** (4), 356–65.

Carlson, R. (1980) Studies of Jungian typology II: representations of the personal world. *Journal of Personality & Social Psychology*, **38** (5), 801–10.

Carlson, R. and Levy, N. (1973) Studies of Jungian typology: memory, social perception and social action. *Journal of Personality*, **41** (4), 559–76.

Carskadon, T.G. (1982) MBTI characterizations: a Jungian horoscope? *Research in Psychological Type*, **5**, 87–8.

Carskadon, T.G. and Cook, D.D. (1982) Validity of MBTI type descriptions as perceived by recipients unfamiliar with type. *Research in Psychological Type*, **5**, 89–94.

Casas, E. (1990) The development of the French version of the MBTI in Canada and in France. *Journal of Psychological Type*, **20**, 3–15.

Cheek, J.M. and Buss, A.H. (1981) Shyness and sociability. *Journal of Personality and Social Psychology*, **41** (2), 330–99.

Ching, M.K.L. (1986) The effect of psychological type upon the composing process of University faculty. *Bulletin of Psychological Type*, **9** (1), 34–7.

Cohen, D. (1976) *Psychologists on Psychology*, Taplinger, New York.

Corlett, E.S. and Millner, N.B. (1993) *Navigating Midlife. Using Typology as a Guide*, Consulting Psychologists Press, Palo Alto, CA.

Costa, P.T. and McCrae, R.R. (1986) Personality stability and its implications for clinical psychology. *Clinical Psychology Review*, **6**, 407–23.

Costa, P.T. and McCrae, R.R. (1992) Normal personality assessment in clinical practice: the NEO Personality Inventory. *Psychological Assessment*, **4** (1), 5–13.

Costa, P.T. and McCrae, R.R. (1994) Set like plaster? Evidence for the stability of adult personality, in *Can Personality Change?* (eds T. Heatherton and J. Weinberger), American Psychological Association, Washington DC.

Costa, P.T. and Widiger, T.A. (eds) (1994) *Personality Disorders and the Five Factor Model of Personality*, American Psychological Association, Washington DC.

Costa, P.T., McCrae, R.R. and Zonderman, A.B. (1987) Environmental and dispositional influences on well-being: longitudinal follow-up of an American national sample. *British Journal of Psychology*, **78**, 299–306.

Davies, H. (1978) Profile of Malcolm Bradbury. *The Sunday Times Magazine*, January 15.

Davis, L.M. (1928) Self-selection of diet by newly weaned infants. *American Journal of Diseases of Children*, **36**, 651–79.

Dean, G. (1986–7) Does astrology need to be true? *The Skeptical Inquirer*, **11**, 166–83, 257–73.

Dean, G. (1992) The bottom line: effect size, in *The Write Stuff: Evaluations of Graphology, the Study of Handwriting Analysis* (eds B. Bayerstein and D. Bayerstein), Prometheus Books, New York.

Dean, G.A., Kelly, I.W., Saklofske, D.H. and Furnham, A. (1992) Graphology and human judgement, in *The Write Stuff: Evaluations of Graphology, the Study of Handwriting Analysis* (eds B. Bayerstein and D. Bayerstein), Prometheus Books, New York.

Dryden, W. and Feltham, C. (1992) *Brief Counselling*, Open University Press, Buckingham.

Duck, S. (1992) *Human Relationships*, 2nd edn, Sage, London.

Dutton, S. (1992) Applications of type to organizational training: revisiting a program design. *Bulletin of Psychological Type*, **15** (3), 4–5.

Epstein, S. (1979) The stability of behaviour. I. On predicting most of the people much of the time. *Journal of Personality and Social Psychology*, **37**, 1097–126.

Erickson, D.B. (1993) The relationship between personality type and preferred counselling model. *Journal of Psychological Type*, **27**, 39–41.

Feingold, A. (1992) Good-looking people are not what we think. *Psychological Bulletin*, **111**, 304–41.

Fleck, D. and Bayne, R. (1990) Psychological type and the design of application forms. *Guidance and Assessment Review*, **6** (6), 2–4.

Forer, B.R. (1949) The fallacy of personal validation: a classroom demonstration. *Journal of Abnormal and Social Psychology*, **44**, 118–23.

Friedman, H.S., Tucker, J.S., Tomlinson-Keasy, C. *et al.* (1993) Does childhood personality predict longevity? *Journal of Personality and Social Psychology*, **65** (1), 176–85.

Frisbie, G.R. (1988) Cognitive styles: an alternative to Keirsey's temperaments. *Journal of Psychological Type*, **16**, 13–21.

Funder, D.C. (1991) Global traits: a neo-Allportian approach to personality. *Psychological Science*, **2**, 31–9.

Funder, D.C. and Sneed, C.D. (1993) Behavioral manifestations of personality: an ecological approach to judgemental accuracy. *Journal of Personality and Social Psychology*, **64** (3), 479–90.

Furnham, A. (1981) Personality and activity preference. *British Journal of Social Psychology*, **20**, 57–68.

Furnham, A. and Schofield, S. (1987) Accepting personality test feedback: a review of the Barnum effect. *Current Psychological Research & Reviews*, **6** (2), 162–78.

Galef, B.G. (1991) A contrarian view of the wisdom of the body as it relates to dietary self-selection. *Psychological Review*, **98** (2), 218–22.

Garden, A.-M. (1985) The effect of Jungian type on burnout. *Journal of Psychological Type*, **10**, 3–10.

Garden, A.-M. (1988) Jungian type, occupation and burnout: an elaboration of an earlier study. *Journal of Psychological Type*, **14**, 2–14.

Garden, A.-M. (1991) Unresolved issues with the Myers–Briggs Type Indicator. *Journal of Psychological Type*, **22**, 3–14.

Garfield, L. (1986) Research on client variables in psychotherapy, in *Handbook of Psychotherapy and Behaviour Change*, 3rd edn (eds L. Garfield and A. Bergin), Wiley, Chichester.

Gébler, E. (1969) *Shall I Eat You Now?* Methuen, London.

Goldberg, L.R. (1992) The development of markers for the big-five factor structure. *Psychological Assessment*, **4** (1), 26–42.

Goldberg, L.R. (1993) The structure of phenotypic personality traits. *American Psychologist*, **48** (1), 26–34.

Gordy, C.C. and Thorne, B.M. (1994) Proof reading ability as a function of personality type. *Journal of Psychological Type*, **28**, 29–36.

Green, D.W. and Wason, P.C. (1982) Notes on the psychology of writing. *Human Relations*, **35** (1), 47–56.

Hammer, A.L. (1985) Psychological type and media preferences in an adult sample. *Journal of Psychological Type*, **10**, 20–6.

Hammer, A.L. (1991) A brief response to the National Research Council's review of the MBTI. Unpublished paper for Consulting Psychologists Press, Palo Alto, CA.

Hammer, A.L. (1993) *Introduction to Type and Careers*, Consulting Psychologists Press, Palo Alto, CA.

Hammer, A.L. and Yeakley, F.R. (1987) The relationship between 'true type' and reported type. *Journal of Psychological Type*, **13**, 52–5.

Hampson, S.E., Gilmour, R. and Harris, P.L. (1978) Accuracy in self-perception: the 'fallacy of personal validation'. *British Journal of Social and Clinical Psychology*, **17**, 231–5.

Harrison, D. and Lawrence, G. (1985) Psychological type and time orientation: do middle school students differ in projecting their personal futures? *Journal of Psychological Type*, **9**, 10–15.

Hartley, J. and Branthwaite, A. (1989) The psychologist as wordsmith: a questionnaire study of the writing strategies of productive British psychologists. *Higher Education*, **18**, 423–52.

Harvey, R.J. and Murray, W.D. (1994) Scoring the Myers–Briggs Type Indicator: empirical comparison of preference score versus latent-trait methods. *Journal of Personality Assessment*, **62** (1), 116–29.

Hayes, J.R. and Flower, L.S. (1986) Writing research and the writer. *American Psychologist*, **41** (10), 1106–13.

Heavrin, A.R. (1992) Careers and occupations column. *Bulletin of Psychological Type*, **15** (2), 17–18.

Herrick, O. (1987) Tailored to your type... . *The Type Reporter*, **2** (4), 11–13.

Hicks, L.E. (1984) Conceptual and empirical analysis of some assumptions of an explicitly typological theory. *Journal of Personality and Social Psychology*, **46** (5), 1118–31.

Hirsh, S.K. (1992) *Using the Myers–Briggs Type Indicator in Organizations*, 2nd edn, Consulting Psychologists Press, Palo Alto, CA.

Hirsh, S.K. and Kummerow, J. (1989) *LifeTypes*, Warner Books, New York.

Hirsh, S.K. and Kummerow, J.M. (1990) *Introduction to Type in Organizations*, 2nd edn, Consulting Psychologists Press, Palo Alto, CA.

Hogan, R., Curphy, G.J. and Hogan, J. (1994) What we know about leadership: effectiveness and personality. *American Psychologist*, **49** (6), 493–504.

Hudson, L. (1968) *Frames of Mind*, Methuen, London.

Jeffries, W.C. (1991) *True to Type*, Hampton Roads, Norfolk, VA.

Jemal, C. (1991) An investigation of shy extraversion according to two aspects of Rowe's theory. Unpublished BSc project, University of East London.

Jensen, G.H. (1987) Learning styles, in *Applications of the Myers–Briggs Type Indicator in Higher Education* (eds J. Provost and S. Anchors), Consulting Psychologists Press, Palo Alto, CA.

Jensen, G.H. and DiTiberio, J.K. (1989) *Personality and the Teaching of Composition*, Ablex Publishing Corporation, Norwood, NJ.

Jung, C.G. (1923) *Psychological Types*, Routledge, London.

Kaplan, M.F. and Singer, E. (1963) Dogmatism and sensory alienation. *Journal of Consulting Psychology*, **27** (6), 486–91.

Keirsey, D. and Bates, M. (1978) *Please Understand Me*, 3rd edn, Prometheus Nemesis, Del Mar, CA.

Kenrick, D. and Funder, D.C. (1988) Profiting from controversy: lessons from the person–situation debate. *American Psychologist*, **43** (1), 23–34.

King, T.J., Thorne, B.M. and Carskadon, T.G. (1993) Psychological type and body weight. *Journal of Psychological Type*, **25**, 39–47.

Kirby, L. (1992) Why type dynamics? *Bulletin of Psychological Type*, **15** (4), 1 and 4.

Kopp, S. (1974) *The Hanged Man*, Science & Behavior Books, Palo Alto, CA.

Krauskopf, C. and Saunders, D.R. (1994) *Personality and Ability: The Personality Assessment System*, University Press of America, London.

Kroeger, O. (1985) Fat is a typological issue. *The Type Reporter*, **1** (3), 16–17.

Kroeger, O. (1991) A day on designing a day. Pre-conference workshop at the IXth APT International Conference, Richmond.

Kroeger, O. and Thuesen, J.M. (1988) *Type Talk*, Delacorte Press, New York.

Kroeger, O. with Thuesen, J.M. (1992) *Type Talk at Work*, Delacorte Press, New York.

Kroeger, O. and Thuesen, J.M. (1994) *16 Ways to Love Your Lover*, Delacorte Press, New York.

Kummerow, J.M. (1988) A methodology for verifying type: research results. *Journal of Psychological Type*, **15**, 20–5.

Kummerow, J.M. (1991) Using the *Strong Interest Inventory* and the *Myers–Briggs Type Indicator* together in career counselling, in *New Directions in Career Planning and the Workplace* (ed. J.M. Kummerow), Consulting Psychologists Press, Palo Alto, CA.

Kummerow, J.M. and McAllister, L.W. (1988) Team-building with the Myers–Briggs Type Indicator: case-studies. *Journal of Psychological Type*, **15**, 26–32.

Kummerow, J.M. and Quenk, N.L. (1992) *Interpretive Guide for the MBTI Expanded Analysis Report*, Consulting Psychologists Press, Palo Alto, CA.

Lambert, M.J., Shapiro, D.A. and Bergin, A.E. (1986) The effectiveness of psychotherapy, in *Handbook of Psychotherapy and Behaviour Change*, 3rd edn (eds L. Garfield and A. Bergin), Wiley, Chichester

Lawrence, G. (1986) Issues in the development of the MBTI. *Journal of Psychological Type*, **12**, 2–7.

Lawrence, G. (1989) Type and stereotype: sorting out the differences. *Bulletin of Psychological Type*, **12** (1), 11–13.

Lawrence, G. (1993) *People Types and Tiger Stripes*, Center for Applications of Psychological Type, Gainesville, FL.

Levesque, M.J. and Kenny, D.A. (1993) Accuracy of behavioural predictions at zero acquaintance: a social relations analysis. *Journal of Personality and Social Psychology*, **65** (6), 1178–87.

Lewis, R. and Lowe, P. (1992) *Individual Excellence: Improving Personal Effectiveness at Work*, Kogan Page, London.

Loftus, E.F. and Klinger, M.R. (1992) Is the unconscious smart or dumb? *American Psychologist*, **47** (6), 761–5.

Lord, W. (1994) Personality tests and interview skills. *Selection and Development Review*, **10** (11), 3–5.

Lowe, P. (1992) Self-awareness: Some issues to debate. *Newsletter of the British Association for Psychological Type*, **3** (5), 4.

Lykken, D.T., McGue, M., Tellegen, A. and Bouchard, T.J. (1992) Emergenesis: genetic traits that may not run in families. *American Psychologist*, **47**, 1565–77.

Macdaid, G. (1988) *Career Choice and MBTI Type* (booklet), Center for Applications of Psychological Type, Gainesville, FL.

Martin, R.P., Underwood, J.R. and Carskadon, T.G. (1985) Psychological type among counsellors of the blind: some anomalous findings. *Journal of Psychological Type*, **9**, 50–7.

McAdams, D.P. (1992) The five-factor model in personality: a critical appraisal. *Journal of Personality*, **60** (2), 329–61.

McBride, M.M. and Martin, G.E. (1988) The relationship between psychological type and preferred counselling theory in graduate counselling students. *Journal of Psychological Type*, **15**, 46–8.

McCarley, N.G. and Carskadon, T.G. (1986) The perceived accuracy of elements of the 16 type descriptions of Myers and Keirsey. *Journal of Psychological Type*, **11**, 2–29.

McCaulley, M. (1992) Asking the right questions. *Bulletin of Psychological Type* (Special issue on leadership), **15** (2), 1 and 5–6.

McCaulley, M.H., Macdaid, G.P. and Kainz, R.I. (1985) Estimated frequencies of the MBTI types. *Journal of Psychological Type*, **9**, 3–9.

McCrae, R.R. (1991) The five factor model and its assessment in clinical settings. *Journal of Personality Assessment*, **57** (3), 399–414.

McCrae, R. (1993) Moderated analyses of longitudinal personality stability. *Journal of Personality and Social Psychology*, **65** (3), 577–85.

McCrae, R. (1993–4) Openness to experience as a basic dimension of personality. *Imagination, Cognition and Personality*, **13** (1), 39–55.

McCrae, R.R. and Costa, P.T. (1989) Re-interpreting the Myers–Briggs Type Indicator from the perspective of the five factor model of personality. *Journal of Personality*, **57** (1), 17–37.

McCrae, R.R. and Costa, P.T. (1991) The NEO Personality Inventory: using the five factor model in counseling. *Journal of Counseling and Development*, **69**, 367–72.

McCrae, R.R. and Costa, P.T. (1993) Conceptions and correlates of openness to experience, in *Handbook of Personality Psychology* (eds S. Briggs, R. Hogan and W. Jones), Academic Press, New York.

McCrae, R.R. and Costa, P.T. (in press) Toward a new generation of personality theories: theoretical contexts for the five factor model, in *The Five-Factor Model of Personality: Theoretical Perspectives* (ed. J. Wiggins), Plenum, New York.

McLuhan, M. (1964) *Understanding Media*, McGraw-Hill, New York.

Miller, T.R. (1991) The psychotherapeutic utility of the five-factor mode of personality: a clinician's experience. *Journal of Personality Assessment*, **57** (3), 415–33.

Murphy, E. (1992) *The Developing Child: Using Jungian Type to Understand Children*, Consulting Psychologists Press, Palo Alto, CA.

Murray, D.G. and Murray, R.R. (1988) *Opposites: When ENFP & ISTJ Interact*, Type Communications, Gladwyne, PA.

Myers, I.B. (1973) Reflections on the history of the Type Indicator. Audio tape of a seminar, edited by Gordon Lawrence.

Myers, I.B. (1976) *Introduction to Type*, 2nd edn, Consulting Psychologists Press, Palo Alto, CA.

Myers, I.B. (1980) *Gifts Differing*, Consulting Psychologists Press, Palo Alto, CA.

Myers, I.B. (1993) *Introduction to Type*, 5th edn (rev. L.K. Kirby and K.D. Myers), Oxford Psychologists Press, Oxford.

Myers, I.B. and McCaulley, M.H. (1985) *Manual: A Guide to the Development and Use of the Myers–Briggs Type Indicator*, Consulting Psychologists Press, Palo Alto, CA.

Myers, K.D. (1987) Katharine C. Briggs and Isabel Briggs Myers: the women behind the MBTI. *Journal of Psychological Type*, **13**, 2–8.

Nicholson, J. (1993) *Men and Women*, Oxford University Press, Oxford.

Nicolson, P. and Bayne, R. (1990) *Applied Psychology for Social Workers*, 2nd edn, Macmillan, London.

Nocita, A. and Stiles, W.B. (1986) Client introversion and counseling session impact. *Journal of Counselling Psychology*, **33** (3), 235–41.

Nolan, L.L. and Patterson, S.J. (1990) The active audience: personality type as an indicator of TV program preference. *Journal of Social Behaviour and Personality*, **5** (6), 697–710.

O'Dell, J.W. (1972) P.T. Barnum explores the computer. *Journal of Consulting and Clinical Psychology*, **38**, 270–3.

Odeluga, K. (1993) Some preliminary steps towards the investigation of implicit relationships between typological (MBTI) functions and reactions to extreme stress. Unpublished BSc project, University of East London.

Ogden, J. (1992) *Fat Chance! The Myth of Dieting Explained*, Routledge, London.

Olson, B. (1993) Is it old age or type development? Type development of a sensor. *Bulletin of Psychological Type*, **16** (4), 3–4.

Oxford Psychologists Press (1993) Reported Type to Best Fit Type: Changes during OPP Qualifying Workshops, Oxford Psychologists Press, Oxford.

Percival, T.Q., Smitheram, V. and Kelly, M. (1992) Myers–Briggs Type Indicator and conflict-handling intention: an interactive approach. *Journal of Psychological Type*, **23**, 10–16.

Perls, F. (1969) *In and Out the Garbage Pail*, Real People Press, Lafayette, CA.

Provost, J.A. (1984) *A Casebook: Applications of the Myers–Briggs Type Indicator in Counseling*, Center for Applications in Psychological Type, Gainesville, FL.

Provost, J.A. (1990) *Work, Play and Type*, Consulting Psychologists Press, Palo Alto, CA.

Provost, J.A., Carson, B.H. with Beidler, P.G. (1987) Teaching excellence and type. *Journal of Psychological Type*, **13**, 23–33.

Quenk, N.L. (1993) *Beside Myself: The Inferior Function in Everyday Life*, Consulting Psychologists Press, Palo Alto, CA.

Rakos, R.F. (1991) *Assertive Behaviour: Theory, Research and Training*, Routledge, London.

Rawling, K. (1994) *Preliminary Manual for the Cambridge Type Inventory*, Unpublished.

Reynierse, J.H. (1993) The distribution and flow of managerial types through organizational levels in business and industry. *Journal of Psychological Type*, **25**, 11–23.

Robertson, I.T. and Kinder, A. (1993) Personality and job competencies: the criterion-related validity of some personality variables. *Journal of Occupational and Organizational Psychology*, **66**, 225–44.

Rogers, C.R. (1961) *On Becoming a Person*, Constable, London.

Rogers, C.R. (1964) Toward a modern approach to values: the valuing process in the mature person. *Journal of Abnormal & Social Psychology*, **68**, 160–7.

Rosenthal, R. (1990) How are we doing in soft psychology? *American Psychologist*, **42** (1), 46–51.

Rosenthal, R. and Rubin, D.B. (1982) A simple, general purpose display of magnitude of experimental effect. *Journal of Educational Psychology*, **74**, 166–9.

Rosenthal, T.L. (1993) To soothe the savage breast. *Behaviour Research and Therapy*, **31** (5), 439–62.

Rowe, D. (1989) *The Successful Self*, Fontana, London.

Ruhl, D.L. and Rodgers, R.F. (1992) The perceived accuracy of the 16 type descriptions of Myers and Keirsey: a replication of McCarley and Carskadon. *Journal of Psychological Type*, **23**, 22–6.

Rytting, M. (1990) Androgynous archetypes: clarifying the relationship between type and archetype. *Journal of Psychological Type*, **20**, 16–24.

Salomone, P.R. (1993) Trade secrets for crafting a conceptual article. *Journal of Counseling and Development*, **72**, 73–6.

Saunders, F.W. (1991) *Katharine and Isabel*, Consulting Psychologists Press, Palo Alto, CA.

Scanlon, S. (1986) A matter of taste ... and type. *The Type Reporter*, **2** (4), 2–10.

Scanlon, S. (1988) Gestures. *The Type Reporter*, **3** (8), 1–4.

Scanlon, S. (1989) What's it like to be a Thinking woman? What's it like to be a Feeling man? *The Type Reporter*, **4** (6), 1–6; (7) 1–6.

Scanlon, S. (1990a) I can't decide what type I am! Part 3 – The PAS. *The Type Reporter*, **5** (4), 1–4.

Scanlon, S. (1990b) Writing YOUR natural way. Part 1 Extraverted or Introvert. Part 2 Sensing or Intuitive. Part 3 Thinking. Part 4 Feeling. Part 5 Perceiving and Part 6 Judging. *The Type Reporter*, **4** (8), 1–6; (9), 1–6; (10), 1–4; (11), 1–4; (12), 1–4 and **5** (1) 1–4.

Scanlon, S. (1991) Relax, Mom, you're doing a great job. Part 1. *The Type Reporter*, **40**, 1–6.

Scanlon, S. (1992) Making love ... What's your style? *The Type Reporter*, **46**, 1–6.

Scanlon, S. (1992–3) Kidtypes. Part 1 Introverts and Extraverts. Part 2 Sensing and

Intuition. Part 3 Thinking and Feeling. Part 4 Judging and Perceiving. *The Type Reporter*, **47**, 1–6; **48**, 1–6; **49**, 1–6: **50**, 1–6.

Scarbrough, D.P. (1993) Psychological types and job satisfaction of accountants. *Journal of Psychological Type*, **25**, 3–10.

Sechrest, L. (1968) Testing, measuring and assessing people, in *Handbook of Personality Theory and Research* (eds E. Borgatta and W. Lambert), Rand McNally, Chicago.

Seegmiller, R.A. and Epperson, D.L. (1987) Distinguishing thinking–feeling preferences through the content analysis of natural language. *Journal of Personality Assessment*, **51** (1), 42–52.

Sellers, S. (ed.) (1991) *Taking Reality By Surprise*, The Women's Press, London.

Sim, H.-S. and Kim, J.-T. (1993) The development and validation of the Korean version of the MBTI. *Journal of Psychological Type*, **26**, 18–27.

Smail, D. (1987) *Taking Care*, Dent, London.

Small, S.A., Zeldin, R.S. and Savin-Williams, R.C. (1983) In search of personality traits: a multimethod analysis of naturally occurring prosocial and dominance behaviour. *Journal of Personality*, **51**, 1–16.

Smith, J.B. (1993) Teachers' grading styles: the languages of Thinking and Feeling. *Journal of Psychological Type*, **26**, 37–41.

Spoto, A. (1989) *Jung's Typology in Perspective*, Sigo Press, Boston.

Spoto, A. (1993) What Jung would be saying about the MBTI and does it even matter? BAPT Annual Conference, Manchester.

Stagner, R. (1958) The gullibility of personnel managers. *Personnel Psychology*, **11**, 347–52.

Stokes, J. (1987a) Exploring the relationship of type and gender. Part 1 Anecdotal experiences of MBTI users. *Journal of Psychological Type*, **13**, 34–43.

Stokes, J. (1987b) Exploring the relationship of type and gender. Part 2 A review and critique of empirical research and other data. *Journal of Psychological Type*, **13**, 44–51.

Storr, A. (1960) *The Integrity of the Personality*, Penguin, Harmondsworth.

Strube, M.J. (1989) Evidence for the *type* in Type A behaviour: a taxometric analysis. *Journal of Personality and Social Psychology*, **56** (6), 972–87.

Thorne, A. (1987) The press of personality: a study of conversations between introverts and extraverts. *Journal of Personality and Social Psychology*, **53**, 718–26.

Thorne, A. and Gough, H. (1991) *Portraits of Type*, Consulting Psychologists Press, Palo Alto, CA.

Van Denburg, T.F. and Kiesler, D.J. (1993) Transactional escalation in rigidity and intensity of interpersonal behaviour under stress. *British Journal of Medical Psychology*, **66**, 15–31.

Walck, C.L. (1992a) The relationship between Indicator type and 'true type': slight preferences and the verification process. *Journal of Psychological Type*, **23**, 17–21.

Walck, C.L. (1992b) Psychological type and management research: a review. *Journal of Psychological Type*, **24**, 13–23.

Ware, R. and Rytting, M. (1989) Identification of J-P preference by viewing interiors of automobiles. *Journal of Psychological Type*, **18**, 63–5.

Widiger, T.A. and Trull, T.J. (1992) Personality and psychopathology: an application of the five-factor model. *Journal of Personality*, **60** (2), 363–93.

Williams, M.Q., Williams, T.F., Qisheng, X. and Xvemei, L. (1992) A glimpse of the psychological types of mainland Chinese undergraduates. *Journal of Psychological Type*, **23**, 3–9.

York, K.L. and John, O.P. (1992) The four faces of Eve: a typological analysis of women's personality at mid-life. *Journal of Personality and Social Psychology*, **63** (3), 494–508.

Zilbergeld, B. (1983) *The Shrinking of America: Myths of Psychological Change*, Little, Boston.

Author index

Subject index